ACCIDENTS

In North American Climbing 2022

Volume 12 | Number 3 | Issue 75

AMERICAN ALPINE CLUB
GOLDEN, COLORADO

ALPINE CLUB OF CANADA
CANMORE, ALBERTA

TECHROCK LIGHT GORE-TEX JACKET

MOUNTAIN TESTED.
ATHLETE TRUSTED.

LAURA DAHLMEIER

MONT BLANC, CHAMONIX, FRANCE

45.8326° N, 6.8652° E

ADIDAS.COM/TERREX

CONTENTS

Front Cover: Dmitriy Litvak descending the exposed Kat Walk on Middle Cathedral Rock in Yosemite Valley. Photo by Dylan Kiyomura.

Back Cover: Mt. Neacola in Alaska, showing the source and approximate expanse of a massive avalanche off the east face. See p.18 for the report. Photo courtesy of Nick Aiello-Popeo.

ISBN: 978-1-7356956-9-3. Printed in South Korea. Published by the American Alpine Club, 710 Tenth Street, Suite 100, Golden, CO, 80401.

WARNING!
The activities described within Accidents in North American Climbing (ANAC)—including but not limited to: rock climbing, ice climbing, mountaineering, backcountry skiing, or any other outdoor activity—carry a significant risk of personal injury or death. The owners, staff, contributors, and volunteers that create this publication recommend that you DO NOT participate in these activities unless you are an expert, have sought or obtained qualified professional instruction or guidance, are knowledgeable about the risks involved, and are willing to assume personal responsibility for all the risks associated with these activities. ANAC and its publisher, the American Alpine Club, MAKE NO WARRANTIES, EXPRESSED OR IMPLIED, OF ANY KIND REGARDING THE CONTENTS OF THIS PUBLICATION, AND EXPRESSLY DISCLAIM ANY WARRANTY REGARDING THE ACCURACY OR RELIABILITY OF INFORMATION CONTAINED HEREIN. The American Alpine Club further disclaims any responsibility for injuries or death incurred by any person engaging in these activities. Use the information contained in this publication at your own risk, and do not depend on the information contained herein for personal safety or for determining whether to attempt any climb, route, or activity described herein. The examples/stories contained herein are anecdotal and/or informational only and are not intended to represent advice, recommendations, or commentary on appropriate conduct, standards or choices that you, the reader, may make regarding your own activities.

ACCIDENTS IN NORTH AMERICAN CLIMBING

Volume 12 | Number 3 | Issue 75

American Alpine Club

EDITOR EMERITUS
John E. (Jed) Williamson

EDITOR
Pete Takeda

DESIGN
David Boersma | Mojave Creative Lab

CONTRIBUTING EDITORS
Aram Attarian (NC), Lindsay Auble (KY and TN),
Dave Weber (AK)

REGIONAL EDITORS
Daniel Apodaca (NM and AZ); Mark Berenblum
(NY); Dan Cousins (New England); Stefani Dawn
(NV); Wren Fournier; Ashton Johnston and Bill
Kinter (CO); Michelle Leber and Sarah Wolfe
(UT); Michael Habicht, Lauren DeLaunay Miller,
and Christy Rosa (CA); Stacia Glenn (WA); Gary
O'Brien (ID and MT); Michael Wejchert (NH)

ADDITIONAL THANKS
Elizabeth Cromwell, Leo Paik, Scott Turpin

AAC EXECUTIVE EDITOR
Dougald MacDonald

Alpine Club of Canada

CANADA EDITOR
Robert Chisnall
anam@alpineclubofcanada.ca

Practi Bolts ®

moveable & reusable
climbing hanger replicas

for climbing instruction
and practice

Practi™
Bolts

NOT FOR
CLIMBING

PREFACE

By Pete Takeda

This is the 75th annual edition of the American Alpine Club's *Accidents* book. For three-quarters of a century, this publication has documented, reported, and analyzed each year's most significant and teachable rock climbing and mountaineering accidents.

This is also my first year as editor in chief. As we close in on publishing the 2022 edition, I can already look back on a rewarding learning curve and look forward to evolving with our ever-changing sport. If climbing mirrors our cultural changes, its accidents are lessons—and cautionary tales. In some cases, mishaps may represent the growth pains of climbing: the pressures of increased participation, expansion of specific genres, and the limited carrying capacity of our outdoor spaces.

There's more to this job than one might assume, so it's a good thing I've been in good hands. AAC Executive Editor Dougald MacDonald—who long helmed *Accidents* as well as the *American Alpine Journal*—made sure I didn't sink under the waves.

Reviewing, editing, and logging scores of accidents brought back memories of my own close calls. I've realized that from my own four decades of climbing experience, there's hardly a single type of accident herein that I am not personally familiar with. These include avalanches, nasty falls, and even having my leg stuck in an offwidth (*just like the guy on page 42*). Whether I've witnessed tragedy, had a close call, or ended up in the hospital, I could, through experience, understand these incidents very well. Over the years I've learned to truly sympathize with those upon whom misfortune has fallen. I've shed real tears these last months for all those affected by climbing mishaps.

I've reminded myself that those who have witnessed or been party to an accident also suffer from the aftermath. They may have an emotional and psychological injury that can be as debilitating as any physical pain. If you are in that position, be gentle with yourself. It's easy to rewrite your recollection in a manner that assigns some responsibility not reflective of the truth of the moment. It takes courage to show kindness to oneself.

It also requires courage for accident victims to speak up. To do so might risk criticism or embarrassment, yet reports like these make a real difference to our community, and you might just save a life.

Finally, thanks to our correspondents, reporters, regional editors, and staff. Without you, this book would not exist.

Submissions

Share your story and help fellow climbers! Visit *publications.americanalpineclub.org* to file an accident report or email us at *accidents@americanalpineclub.org*.

Friends of Accidents in North American Climbing

The following people and companies contributed $100 or more in 2021 specifically to *Accidents*. Thank you! Make your contribution at *americanalpineclub.org/donate*.

adidas Outdoor	Kyle Emert	Kevin Smith
Laura Chedalawada	Carla Firey	Brian Steers
Denver Climbing Company	Richard Hoffman, M.D.	Mimi Stone
Desert Mountain Medicine	Jonathan Hough	Doug Wilson
Charlie Eiriksson	Myung-Jin Oh	Sara & Owen Zacharias

Protect yourself.

The AAC is the largest community of climbers in the country, and our members take pride in advocating for the public lands and conservation policies that protect wild landscapes and the wild people who love them. Join us in this mission— and simultaneously ensure you have the emergency rescue and medical expense coverage you need to dream big.

Ready to up your commitment to the AAC's advocacy work, and looking for 100% peace of mind in the backcountry? Consider upgrading your membership today. Learn more about the Club and join or renew at americanalpineclub.org.

United We Climb.

American Alpine Club

James Saarela contemplates a nighttime descent from The Thumb in Little Cottonwood Canyon, Utah. Sometimes the true crux of a day comes while trying to get down safely. *James Burson*

Know the Ropes
NAVIGATING APPROACHES & DESCENTS
BY STEFANI DAWN & CODY BRADFORD

In smaller rock climbing areas, botching the approach and descent can be annoying. In large or complex terrain—such as Red Rock Canyon, Yosemite Valley, or Joshua Tree—not knowing the approach and descent beta can not only ruin your day, but also significantly increase your accident risk.

Climbers often spend a lot of time planning for the route itself: Which climb? What gear do I need? How hard is it? But in many locations, a significant portion of the "climb" is the approach and descent.

Similarly, much of the guidebook or online information about climbing areas is devoted to the routes themselves as opposed to the approaches and descents. Approach and descent information is often vague and general, leaving you to ascertain the finer details on your own. And these "details," or lack thereof, can keep you from reaching your destination and increase your risk. A surprisingly large number of search and rescue (SAR) responses reported in ANAC are attributable to strandings and falls during approaches and descents.

When a climb's approach, ascent, or descent takes too long, it's easy to rush, tempting us to skip or miss key safety steps or take shortcuts. Off-trail shortcuts not only can damage sensitive land, they also can take us into more dangerous territory with drop-offs, steep and loose soil, or boulder/scree fields. As an example in this edition, a climber got cliffed out and nearly benighted while attempting to retreat near the end of the Rundle Traverse in Alberta (see page 106) and wisely requested a rescue.

Climbers may fall into the trap of safety-related shortcuts with mindsets like: "Just this once" or "The chances are slim something will go wrong" or "I've done this before, and it's not a problem." In 2020, for example, two climbers realized they took the wrong gully on the way to Solar Slab in Red Rock Canyon. They were unroped on exposed 4th- and low 5th-class terrain. Because they had done this type of climbing before, at their home crag of Seneca Rocks in West Virginia, they decided to down-climb instead of rappel to get back on the correct approach as quickly as possible. One of the climbers then fell approximately 40 feet, breaking multiple bones and becoming unconscious, requiring an airlift. Fortunately, he was wearing a helmet, which possibly saved his life.

It is not uncommon for climbing accidents to occur on descents. After the main event, we are tired. It's easy to enter into an "it's done" mindset and let down our guard. But, the terrain can still be difficult, often more challenging than expected, and there may be limited daylight at this point. The reason why people would want to beat the dark is understandable, especially when having to do an unfamiliar walk-off, but rushing can lead to errors.

In this article, we share some tips to help navigate approaches and descents to save time and reduce risk. These generally are focused on multi-pitch climbs, single-day alpine adventures, or single-pitch crags with lengthy or complicated approaches. But many tips apply to a wide variety of climbing adventures. Even popular and well-trafficked areas like Eldorado Canyon in Colorado have challenging and potentially dangerous descents.

If you get lost on the approach and arrive late to the climb, perhaps the number one tip is to be willing to forgo the climb. That can be a difficult decision, especially when you are on your one big climbing trip of the year and have specific objectives. But the decision to forgo a climb is often easier when it is part of the overall plan and when backup options are in place.

PLANNING TIPS

Pick an appropriate route. Choose an adventure that is within your experience level. Is it your first multi-pitch climb? Maybe pick a well-trafficked route with a straight-forward approach/descent and adequate cell service. You may have to wait in line, but at least you will have people around if you need help! Try hiring a guide service if you are new to an area or unsure if your experience is adequate for a particular adventure. You can even tell the guide service that one of your goals is to get better at navigating the approach or descent, finding the route, and learning bail techniques and options.

Do your research. Read multiple sources of beta ahead of time and take notes to bring with you. Review and compare guidebooks if there is more than one for

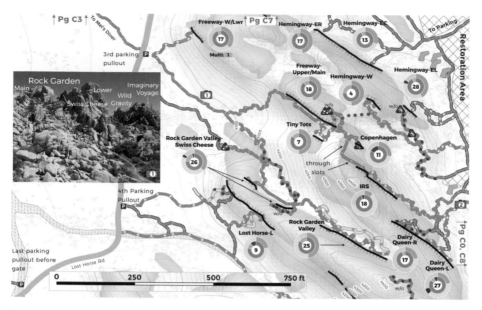

To stay on the right path in complex terrain, look for small-scale, climbing-specific maps, topos, and marked-up pictures, often found in guidebooks or online. This small-scale (1:1,500) map shows part of Joshua Tree National Park and includes a perspective picture and other tools to help orient climbers. *Climb-On Maps*

the area. If your climbing objective is on Mountain Project or another online guide, read everything about the climb, including the comments. Look for specific, helpful descriptions and distill the beta. Comments can be a fantastic source of information—you may discover where other people had issues or were misled by incorrect or incomplete beta.

Gather and study visual guides to help you navigate the approach and descent. For macro-level navigation, get or download maps and study them well. Take screenshots of satellite images. Have resources on paper or available offline, so you are prepared if you don't have cell service. For micro-level navigation (technical or quasi-technical terrain), look for perspective pictures, topos, maps, and diagrams to help you identify the correct path. Maybe someone took a picture of that "obvious boulder" that you can take with you to help you find it.

If it's likely that you'll run into 4th- or 5th-class climbing on the approach or descent, know how to and be prepared to protect exposed climbing. See the "Know the Ropes" article in ANAC 2018 (available at publications.americanalpineclub.org) for lots of helpful ideas.

Be realistic with your plan. Create a plan that has realistic time estimates. Time estimates in guidebooks are often created by people that know exactly where they are going and what they are doing. Double (or even triple) estimated times for the approach, the climb, and the descent, especially if the area is new to you, the area is large and complex, or if a climb is popular and you could end up getting stuck behind a slow party. If your timing is significantly off from your estimate during any part of the day, reassess and be willing to retreat.

Having a backup plan that includes less committing climbing can be helpful. If your big multi-pitch objective gets nixed because of approach problems, a backup with fun, easily accessible single-pitch climbs might make you more willing to walk away from Plan A.

Don't forget to consider all of your options. If there is a nontechnical approach or descent option, such as a hiking trail, it might be worth taking, even if it is considerably longer on paper. On easier terrain, you will likely move faster, and it's often less frustrating and tiring, saving mental and physical energy.

Determine current conditions. Be sure to consider the weather, the time of year, and the sun/shade orientation of the climb, the approach, and the walk-off. For example, a slab can quickly turn slick in the rain, and snow and ice can remain in shady areas. Joining active social media groups for climbers in a given area can be a great way to find out about recent trips and conditions of climbs. If possible, consider taking a day to scope out the approach and even try to backtrack the walk-off during daylight ahead of a big climb. Taking photos and notes can be helpful.

You can also visit or reach out to a local outfitter or climbing organization

"During an approach in the North Cascades, my partner and I tried to force the terrain to match our beta and ended up leaving the valley far too early, adding two difficult hours to our approach. Before each critical route-finding decision, slow down and study all available clues. If what you're seeing doesn't match your route description, keep looking before committing." —*Dougald MacDonald*

to ask about current conditions. In April 2022, a pair of climbers visited the Strawberry Station General Store, a local outfitter at Lover's Leap in California. This area was devastated by the Caldor fire in the fall of 2021 and had just reopened. The staff of local climbers informed the visitors of recent changes to the descent trail, which helped them safely navigate down from the climb without causing further damage to the area. The visiting climbers also inquired about ways to support the recovery. It's nice to donate/contribute to the climbing areas you frequent!

Inform others of your plan. Especially for remote climbs with limited cell service, it is essential to inform people of your plan (and backup plans). Provide them with specifics on the route, approach, and descent and when they should call for help. Stick to your plan: If a rescue is needed, SAR can use that plan to reduce search times.

APPROACH AND DESCENT NAVIGATION TIPS

Whether digital or paper, have your maps, photos, and notes with you. Refer to them as often as needed and keep an open mind. Does the trail you're taking *really* match the description? It can be easy to make any path fit the description to convince yourself that you are on the right track. Don't be afraid to turn around if you feel you are heading down the wrong way. Often, our gut instinct is not that far off, especially for those who climb a lot.

Look for clues that show you are on the right track, such as key terrain features, cairns, flagging, worn paths, rappel anchors, etc. Be aware that terrain features look different from various angles, cairns may have been mistakenly placed off route, and "worn paths" may be animal trails. Continuous reassessment with your navigation resources is essential.

Resist taking shortcuts. Many accidents are attributable to people wanting a quicker, more direct path. If there was an easier option, that would be the beta!

In complex, loose, or exposed terrain, it's a good idea to wear your helmet during approaches and descents in case of rockfall or an uncontrolled slip. And this one we all know but sometimes sacrifice to our detriment: rest, eat, and drink water.

GETTING STUCK

Hopefully, with planning, research, and appropriate equipment, getting stranded or stuck is not in your future. But it is important to recognize when you are lost or stuck and need to reassess. If you've lost critical equipment (e.g., your rope, as in the case of two climbers trying to rappel off Castleton Tower last year—see page 84) or are unable to continue safely, a rescue may be necessary. Being ready to spend the night outside is an important precaution. Many rescues are only required because climbers tried to navigate a descent in the dark when they should have hunkered down and waited until the morning. One possibly avoidable rescue occurred on the Grand Teton last summer when a team was benighted while carrying insufficient clothing (see page 93).

MACRO-NAVIGATION TOOLS

With offline capabilities, apps like Mountain Project, Gaia, and Google Maps have become popular with climbers for macro-level navigation. Many climbers rely solely on technology's help, which is sufficient in many cases. But it is important to recognize the limitations of digital technology in wilderness terrain. GPS accuracy can be impacted in some areas, especially those with canyons, high cliffs, and dense trees. Treat the blue dot as an approximation (which can help identify general "vicinity") and always use good judgment.

Analog resources can be a powerful tool when used in combination with digital. Paper maps and an analog compass have numerous advantages, including not running out of battery power and the ability to spread the map out in a large visual field to more easily orient it (and yourself) with the terrain. If you are not an avid map and compass user, consider working on these skills and including a paper map and compass in your pack as a backup.

where am I? where am i going? how do i get there?

Navigation Resources

Do Your Research!

Research the approach, route, and descent before leaving.

Climbing beta sites <
Local websites <
Social media groups <

> Guidebooks
> Climber maps/topos
> Park/Trail maps

Website comments can have a wealth of info!

Macro-level navigation

Micro-level navigation

think...
> 4th-class approach
> Descending a ridgeline/narrow canyon
> Finding the rappel location

gather and study:
· detailed maps/topos
· marked-up pictures
· written directions
· climber comments
✗ Note identifiable landmarks and specific gear requirements.

'blue dot' apps/gps devices

· Gives a general location.
· Depends on satellite coverage.
· Easy to zoom beyond intended scale.
· Diminished by features (mountains, trees, cliffs, canyons, etc.) that block/reflect signal.

paper map and compass

· Dependent on compass skills.
· Difficult without view of landmarks.
· Challenging during storms and at night.
· Always displays at intended scale.

ACCURACY

SCALE Digital and analog maps need to be at an appropriate scale to be useful. Find 1:10,000 or smaller for complex terrain.

· Great visual reference.
· Angles of imagery can distort features.
· Non-urban imagery can be outdated/inaccurate.

SATELLITE IMAGERY

· Published maps are rarely displayed with satellite imagery.
· Feature data are displayed with intuitive symbols.

Treat the blue dot as approximate and use terrain features as clues!

In your pack

DIGITAL DEPENDENT

· Download appropriate apps/maps.
  > Make sure they're available offline!
· Take photos of paper maps/guidebooks.
· Take photos of or type beta notes.
· Don't forget a backup battery source!

Consider bringing map/compass and print backups of important info.

Consider downloading offline apps and maps.

ARDENT ANALOG

· Have your map and compass.
· Bring guidebooks or photocopies.
· Take hard-copy beta notes.
· Print guidance/photos from online sources.
· Weatherproof critical items.

In other cases, self-rescue knowledge can keep you from getting stuck and allow you to reverse course. After realizing he was off route while rappelling off the summit of Devils Tower in Wyoming, a climber last year successfully ascended the rope back to the top so he and his partner could find the correct rappel (see page 96). If you are going on a multi-pitch adventure, you will want to be proficient in techniques like escaping a belay or rappel and ascending the rope(s). Practicing these skills regularly in a safe environment will help you perform them effectively and efficiently if the need arises.

Your goal should be self-sufficiency, but you shouldn't hesitate to call for help if you genuinely need it or to prevent a bad situation from worsening. Call 911 (or text in low-service areas), and they will dispatch the appropriate rescue team. Prioritize the critical information: where you are, what you were doing, the severity of the situation and any injuries, and your name. Be familiar with how to find your GPS coordinates on your phone or satellite communicator. Look for terrain features that can help searchers identify where you are. If you have a compass, use it to determine the direction of those features. For remote adventures with limited cell service, invest in a satellite-based two-way emergency communication device such as SPOT X or inReach. Just know that it may be hours before SAR can safely respond, so always pack an efficient but well-stocked first aid and emergency kit.

For most North American climbing areas, SAR teams offer assistance at no cost, but you may be charged if medical transportation is required or if the fire department gets involved. American Alpine Club members receive various rescue benefits (depending on membership level), which can cover some transportation costs and limited emergency medical care for backcountry accidents. While initiating a rescue, members should contact Redpoint Travel Protection (+1-628-251-1510) immediately, if possible. More details on the rescue benefits' procedures and limitations are at americanalpineclub.org/rescue. Other insurance options may be available for certain situations. Be sure to understand all the terms and conditions of your policy.

It is easy to get excited by a climbing objective and focus most of our attention on the beta for the climb itself. But if we don't adequately prepare to navigate the approach and descent, we risk never making it there or even getting injured on unknown terrain. Almost every climber has a story about an approach gone awry or an epic walk-off. With proper research and planning, your stories will be about the amazing climb. No one will want to hear about the boring, went-exactly-as-planned approach and descent.

Stefani Dawn is a Las Vegas–based ANAC regional editor and co-owner of Climb-On Maps (climbonmaps.com) with her husband, Rick Momsen. Together they've walked over 1,700 miles, sometimes in quite dangerous terrain, to map approaches and walk-offs for climbs in four large climbing areas in the western United States. Momsen, with 20 years of geographic information system experience, also contributed to this article.

Cody Bradford is an AMGA-certified rock guide in Salt Lake City, Utah. Passionate about climber education, Bradford runs accounts on YouTube and Instagram (@thecodybradford) that share concepts and tools to meet climbing problems with unique and simple solutions.

ESSENTIALS

WHAT TO BRING

The following packing considerations may help deal with complex or unknown approaches or descents, or with emergencies that might arise:

- *Appropriate footwear.* In Red Rock Canyon, a light pair of sticky rubber approach shoes (with sufficient tread) may be adequate, but in the North Cascades of Washington, shoes likely will need better traction (e.g., lug soles) and water resistance.
- *Traction.* Is there a chance you'll encounter snow or ice? You may want to pack gaiters, Microspikes/crampons, and an ice axe. A fatality last year on Mt. Olympus in Utah resulted from the absence of an ice axe or crampons during the approach to a long, moderate rock climb (see page 83).
- *Retreat gear.* Extra slings, carabiners, rap rings, and "throw-away" gear like old nuts can be used to back up old rappel stations or set up your own anchors.
- *Twin/half ropes or a tagline.* Carrying two ropes provides redundancy in case a rope gets stuck. Plus, it doubles the rappel length, saving time or ensuring you don't run out of rope on a long rappel.
- *Climbing pack.* If you won't be passing by the base of the route on the descent—or aren't sure—carry a backpack small enough to be comfortable for climbing but large enough to fit necessities: headlamp, clothing layers, food, water, and shoes. To save room inside while approaching or descending, you can wear your harness and helmet and secure the rope(s) tightly and neatly to the backpack.
- *Approach pack.* If you know you will be returning to (or near) the base of the route, consider using an "approach pack" that is comfortable and can easily carry gear and extra supplies.
- *During a technical approach/descent:* Consider stacking one of the ropes in your backpack, allowing you to pull out rope quickly for a short belay. Learn to "Kiwi coil" your rope to shorten it while moving together. Wear your helmet and harness in tricky terrain, in case you need to rope up; putting on a harness can be difficult or dangerous in exposed spots. On your harness, only carry what you expect to use—dangling too much stuff from gear loops increases the likelihood of gear getting hung up or lost. Useful items to keep on the harness may include: a 48-inch sewn sling; a sling, cordage, or pre-sewn friction wrap like the HollowBlock; several locking carabiners; and a plaquette-style belay/rappel device (e.g., ATC Guide or Reverso). Keep cams and other protection readily accessible in your pack.
- *Two-way radios* (walkie talkies) facilitate critical communication during a climb or on unknown rappels. They can also let you and your partner briefly split up and scope different descent or approach options.
- *Nighttime gear.* For long routes or remote areas, be prepared to navigate after dark with a bright headlamp and extra batteries. Also be ready to spend a night outside if necessary by bringing insulating and weatherproof layers, emergency shelter (such as a bothy bag or tarp), lighter, a whistle (to attract rescuers), extra food and water, and a backup battery for your phone.

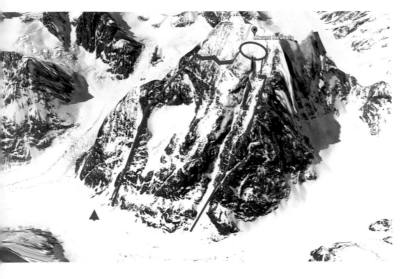

ALASKA

AVALANCHE
Neacola Mountains

Less than two weeks prior to completing the first ascent of the 4,600-foot north face of Mt. Neacola (5.10 A2 M6), a trio of New Hampshire-based climbers were nearly killed in an avalanche.

On April 1, I (31), Ryan Driscoll (34), and Justin Guarino (32) landed via ski-wheel airplane on the remote Lobster Claw Glacier below the east face of Mt. Neacola (ca. 9,350 feet). Deep snow caused our bush pilot to drop us off about a quarter-mile farther down-glacier than during our first attempt on the mountain in 2019. As luck would have it, this probably saved our lives.

At around 4:30 a.m. on April 4, serac fall high on Neacola triggered a deep slab avalanche with a crown line estimated at eight feet high and 2,000 feet across. The three of us were sound asleep in separate tents in base camp, waiting out yet another storm after caching climbing gear at the base of the north face. In the blackness, we were awoken by a loud noise just one second before being lofted—in our tents—into the night sky. Death appeared to be just moments away, and I felt a sense of disappointment rather than real fear. The avalanche instantly crushed our tents around our bodies as we were hurled through the air. After the initial air blast subsided, we briefly decelerated. This allowed for a glimmer of hope we might survive. But any hope was quickly dashed as a second powerful wave of energy (which we assume was avalanche debris) swept us further across the glacier.

In the end, all three of us survived the avalanche with minor injuries, such as a sprained neck and chest pain. We had been blasted horizontally about 300 feet. A snow picket that had been sitting in the snow had somehow passed through the wall of my tent and completely through my sleeping bag. Though we weren't badly hurt, our entire base camp had been erased. As the blizzard continued unabated, we found ourselves lacking tents, food, boots—everything was gone. Furthermore, the weather prevented us from moving our camp or even digging a snow cave. We braced a broken tent into place and huddled inside. At dawn, we walked forlornly across the snow, picking up scattered pieces of food or supplies. One heavy duffel bag was found a half-mile down the glacier, on the far side of a tall moraine.

For two stressful days, we suffered in our destroyed camp as the wind and snow pummeled us. Falling asleep in the same location was quite stressful. In the whiteout, it was impossible to see what other avalanche hazard remained overhead—not that we wanted to know. My neck was badly sprained, so Ryan and Justin suffered greatly to retrieve our heavy cache of gear from below the north face during the storm. Fifty-two hours after the avalanche, the weather improved and our bush pilot was able to retrieve us. Eleven days later, we returned and completed the first ascent of the north face of Mt. Neacola.

ANALYSIS

Essentially, the entire 6,500-foot-tall east face of Neacola avalanched into the one-third-mile-wide valley where we were camped. As experienced mountaineers, guides, and avalanche educators, all three of us were well aware of the hazards that one faces on an alpine climbing expedition in a remote area. However, exploratory alpinism in big mountains requires a risk tolerance that far exceeds what one would consider acceptable at the crag or even in the mountains in the Lower 48.

In 2019 we were surprised by how tight the valleys in the Neacola Mountains were compared with the Central Alaska Range (including Denali National Park). However, during storms in 2019, none of the many natural avalanches affected our camp. This may have caused complacency in 2021.

In a relatively unexplored area, there is no communal history to inform decisions. For example, the West Buttress Route on Denali has avalanche hazard. But tens of thousands of climbers have been able to pass down their experiences, allowing today's mountaineers to make better decisions.

The small likelihood of a monster serac-triggered avalanche (as we experienced) was weighed against the difficulty of moving our base camp even farther away from the bush pilot's landing zone. It was also weighed against our desire to explore a remote area and try a huge, unclimbed big wall. In the end, we knew the hazards and we accepted the risk. We almost paid with our lives. (Source: Nick Aiello-Popeo.)

Editor's Note: See the 2022 American Alpine Journal for Ryan Driscoll's feature article about the attempts on and first ascent of the north face (a.k.a. the "Medusa Face") of Mt. Neacola.

Ryan Driscoll standing behind Nick Aiello-Popeo's destroyed tent. The red tent was nearly ruined, but the team sheltered inside of it. *Justin Guarino*

FATAL CREVASSE FALL
Denali National Park, Eldridge Glacier

On May 1, a 23-year-old female and 28-year-old male flew onto the South Spur of the Eldridge Glacier with the intent of exploring ski mountaineering objectives in the vicinity. This spur of the Eldridge Glacier originates to the northeast of the Ruth Amphitheater, and is a broad basin comprised of heavily glaciated terrain. Given these conditions, the team was equipped for glacier travel. They wore harnesses while skiing, and each skier had a 30-meter rope in his/her pack.

The ski partners had spent most of the day on May 2 skiing on terrain in close proximity to their camp. They awoke on May 3 to clear and calm conditions and planned for a similar day of skiing further from their camp location. The pair had already skied a few different runs when the accident occurred.

At approximately 3:10 p.m., the male skier was breaking trail on a 20° slope with roughly 20 cm of unconsolidated new snow. The female skier was spaced 15 to 20 yards behind the male when he fell through a snow bridge that suddenly collapsed. The skiers were unroped at the time of the fall. The female partner approached the lip of the newly exposed crevasse but was unable to see nor get a verbal response from the male skier. At 3:21 p.m., she activated the SOS feature on her Garmin inReach satellite device along with the message: "a skier in crevasse unresponsive."

Denali mountaineering rangers launched their rescue helicopter with two rangers on board at 4:02 p.m. from Talkeetna. This initial response team arrived on scene at 4:33 p.m. The helicopter then returned to Talkeetna for additional NPS personnel.

The initial priorities for the ranger team on scene were assessment of the surviving skier and accessing the patient in the crevasse. These tasks were handled concurrently, and once an anchor system was constructed, one ranger was lowered into the crevasse. The male patient was located approximately 100 feet below the surface on a hard ice floor. The ranger reported no signs of life and at 5 p.m. confirmed the patient was deceased.

The ranger was hauled out of the crevasse to both inform the partner of his findings and for further planning. At this time, the helicopter had returned with two additional rangers. One ranger remained on scene to assist with the recovery operation, and one ranger accompanied the surviving skier back to Talkeetna.

ANALYSIS
All glaciated terrain demands respect. This pair of skiers did many things well to prepare for their trip and their chosen destination. They discussed route planning, emergency plans, and equipment choices. But still, the hidden dangers of crevasses remain. Roping up, especially during uphill travel, is an additional layer of safety when traveling in these environments. Both climbing and skiing teams should stack many factors in their favor to create the largest safety margins possible.

Even with proper equipment and rescue preparation, the totality of the circumstances during an accident may prove overwhelming. In these instances, it is best to stay safe, to call for help, and to stay put. This is the exact plan followed by the female skier, and these actions may have prevented further tragedy that afternoon. (*Source: Denali Mountaineering Rangers.*)

FALLING ICE | Fatality
Denali, West Face of Reality Ridge

On May 13, Denali mountaineering rangers received an SOS message from a Garmin inReach satellite device. At 6:01 a.m., rangers began two-way communications with a climbing party comprised of Climber 1 (male, 31) and Climber 2 (male, 32). These climbers had been approaching the base of a climb on the west face of Reality Ridge on Denali when a large icefall released above them.

The reporting party (Climber 1) stated that he had sustained a head injury and that his climbing partner (Climber 2) had been killed after being hit by the falling ice and the subsequent avalanche. An initial helicopter response team of two rangers arrived on scene at 8:17 a.m.

Climber 1 was located from the air, and the team was able to land at his location. The patient was loaded into the helicopter and further assessed for injuries. Due to both direct observation of the deceased climber from the air and overhead serac hazard on scene, the decision was made to first transport the head injury patient to an awaiting medical helicopter and then return for a recovery operation. The helicopter arrived in Talkeetna at 9:01 a.m. Climber 1 was treated for multiple traumatic injuries and flown to definitive care in Anchorage via medical helicopter.

The red circle marks the accident site below Reality Ridge on Denali's southeast side. Significant icefall in such terrain may occur with no rhyme or reason. This team had planned well but experienced very bad luck. *NPS Photo*

Inclement weather prevented further recovery efforts for the remainder of May 13. On May 14, a team of two rangers departed in the helicopter for a recovery attempt. Due to the serac hazard on scene, a helicopter short-haul was selected as the preferred method, in order to expose the least number of personnel to potential hazards for the least amount of time. This team completed the extrication from avalanche debris and a short-haul recovery by 11:30 a.m.

ANALYSIS

All climbers confront both subjective and objective hazards each time they rope up. Climbers can mitigate as many of these factors as possible and yet still be vulnerable to hazards that are outside of their control. This team was moving efficiently through the terrain during early morning hours, when rock, snow, and ice generally is predicted to be the most stable (i.e., frozen). Good planning and open communication were reported by this team. They were unfortunately in the wrong place at the wrong time. (*Source: Denali Mountaineering Rangers.*)

FROSTBITE | Poor Position
Denali, West Buttress

On the afternoon of May 22, two male climbers left 14,200-foot camp for 17,200-foot camp. The 57-year-old male and 56-year-old male embarked on their climb in spite of weather warnings from rangers and during winds gusting to 40 mph in camp. After a mountaineering ranger explained that wind speeds would be much greater on the ridge above the fixed lines, one climber responded by saying, "The wind doesn't bother us." NPS personnel observed the team proceed to take roughly seven hours to ascend the fixed lines. [*Editor's Note: This section typically takes about two hours to get to the lines and another hour to ascend them.*]

The team was forced to make camp on the exposed ridge before reaching 17,200-foot camp. During the overnight hours, wind destroyed the team's tent. The team abandoned their camp and equipment and retreated to 14,200-foot camp on the afternoon of May 23. (The high winds later blew their abandoned backpacks off the ridge.) The team arrived at the NPS tent and requested assistance at 4:55 p.m. The 57-year-old male had sustained frostbite injuries to all fingers on his right hand except for the thumb. NPS personnel assessed, rewarmed, and treated all injuries.

Due to their lack of remaining equipment and the fact that their injuries would prevent adequate self-arrest, this team was evacuated off the mountain on May 24. They were flown to 7,200-foot camp, from which they were able to fly with an air taxi service to Talkeetna.

ANALYSIS
Historically, frostbite injuries account for over 25 percent of the patients treated by the NPS on Denali. Despite preventive educational efforts prior to all Denali climbs, the NPS continues to see debilitating frostbite injuries each season. The high altitude, dynamic storm systems, and arctic cold conditions combine to exacerbate the precursors that lead to cold injury. No climbing day or summit attempt is worth losing body parts.

Climbers must take active steps to warm any cold body parts prior to continuing an ascent. The human body has an extremely difficult time rewarming itself after being overcome by the ambient temperatures and wind chill on Denali. (*Source: Denali Mountaineering Rangers and the Editors.*)

ACCIDENTAL SOS ACTIVATION
Denali, West Buttress

In the early morning hours of May 29, Denali mountaineering rangers were notified of an SOS activation at 11,200-foot camp. Ranger teams on the mountain at the 7,200, 7,800, and 14,200-foot camps were notified and involved in the information gathering process.

Over the next two hours, rangers at these locations made numerous attempts to contact climbing parties at 11,200-foot camp via radio. Talkeenta incident command was able to track down the device owner and his group information. Talkeetna personnel were also able to contact the owner's wife and initiate two-way communication with the device. At 2 a.m., the owner made contact and reported that it was indeed an accidental SOS alert.

ANALYSIS

The prevalence of satellite-based communication devices has increased exponentially in recent years. These devices have both advantages and disadvantages. The main advantages include the rapid deployment of rescue resources when the SOS feature is utilized, the transmission of the incident location, and (for most devices used today) two-way communication capability with rescue teams.

The primary disadvantages are the overuse of the SOS feature for non-emergent circumstances and the issue presented in this incident report—false activation. The latter occurs primarily through user error, and it unnecessarily puts a vast array of resources into motion. It is important for all device owners to know their equipment well, protect their devices from accidental SOS activation, and to only utilize the SOS feature in emergency circumstances requiring outside assistance. (*Source: Denali Mountaineering Rangers.*)

HIGH ALTITUDE PULMONARY EDEMA | Ascending Too Fast
Denali, West Buttress

On May 29, a 25-year-old male climber was assisted to the NPS medical tent at 14,200-foot camp by his climbing partners. The team reported they had flown to 7,200-foot camp and immediately moved to 11,200-foot camp. They then spent two nights at that elevation before moving to 14,200-foot camp on May 28. This climber had become increasingly short of breath at rest and lethargic since arriving at camp. The patient also reported having taken nifedipine, a rescue medication for climbers suffering from high altitude pulmonary edema (HAPE), prophylactically during his entire expedition.

NPS personnel assessed and treated this climber for HAPE for two days, until the weather became suitable for a helicopter evacuation. Upon arrival in Talkeetna, the patient was transferred to local ambulance. Given his vast improvement upon descent to an elevation of 350 feet above sea level in town, he was able to refuse transport.

ANALYSIS

In recent seasons, Denali mountaineering rangers have observed a wide range of tactics to subvert the effects of altitude. Altitude chambers, prior acclimatization on other peaks, and medications have all been utilized to circumvent spending the requisite time on Denali. Some climbers are able to adjust to the altitude and get off the mountain quickly enough before signs and symptoms of altitude illness occur. However, more often than not, these tactics are unsuccessful. The rangers often see expeditions fail early or see patients get sick from going too high too quickly.

Prophylactic medication use is one of the more disturbing trends rangers have observed as it often enables climbers to ascend beyond their natural readiness and then suffer a rapid onset of symptoms. In addition, these same altitude illness medications are often rendered less effective when used to treat individuals who have been utilizing them prophylactically. (*Source: Denali Mountaineering Rangers.*)

ARIZONA

LOOSE ROCK AT BASE OF ROUTE
Phoenix, South Mountain Preserve

On November 11, Joshua Brown (23) and a partner (22) were climbing in an undeveloped area that required 3rd- and 4th-class scrambling up a loose slope to access the base of the crag. The pair finished a ground-up, trad first ascent and began packing to hike out in the dark. As they did so, a microwave oven–size granite boulder dislodged from a rock pile next to the belay stance. The boulder landed atop Brown's foot. As a climbing guide with an EMT-B certification, Brown quickly assessed his injury as a fractured metatarsal.

It took about an hour to descend the slope and hike the one mile back to the car, during which Brown suffered secondary injuries (abrasions and lacerations) from falling several times.

ANALYSIS
Brown is a very experienced climber and guide. He and his partner (a professional climber with 10 years of experience) are proficient desert adventurers and aware of the risks of climbing in an undeveloped area. While they were concerned about loose rock in the belay area, the block that fell on Brown's foot appeared solid, and in fact they had used it as a place to sit. "We overestimated (the block's) stability, as it managed to dislodge from just walking below it," Brown said. Physically testing the rock likely would have revealed the hazard: "I'm confident that us trying to move it would have made its instability apparent." (*Source: Joshua Brown.*)

GROUND FALL | Improperly Clipped Anchor Tether
Cochise Stronghold, Owl Rock

On the afternoon of January 31, Tim Parker (35) suffered a ground fall from the anchors of Naked Prey (5.12a) in Cochise Stronghold. Parker is a climber with over 15 years of experience. His partner, Darcy Mullen (32), is a climber of over 10 years. They are both mountaineering instructors for an international outdoor education organization.

The pair had decided to finish their day with several pitches on Owl Rock, a pinnacle with several high-quality one-pitch routes. Mullen led Nightstalker (5.9), a classic mixed gear/bolt route on the lower-angle front side of Owl Rock. She built an anchor and belayed Parker to the top.

Mullen rappelled the overhanging backside of the pinnacle, passing over the line of Naked Prey. Parker then rigged the two-bolt anchor with a quad cordelette in order to top-rope Naked Prey, and Mullen lowered him to the base of the climb. He then top-roped the route. Back on top, Parker decided it made more sense to rappel than be lowered due to the location of the anchor bolts.

For an anchor tether, he used a double-length sewn nylon runner girth-hitched

Reconstruction of the anchor atop Owl Rock. The climber first clipped in with the end of his tether sling (left). He then tried to shorten his tether by clipping a shorter loop created by an overhand knot tied in the sling. However, he failed to capture the shorter loop (right). Under load, the knot initially jammed in the base of the carabiner. It temporarily held his weight, but then pulled through. *Tim Parker*

around both hard points on his harness. Parker had pre-rigged the tether with two overhand knots, dividing the sling into three segments to allow for various clip-in points and for extending his rappel device. He used a locking carabiner to clip the tether into the shelf of the cordelette anchor. Unbeknownst to him, the carabiner was not properly clipped to his tether, but this fact would not be revealed for a moment. Parker did a visual double-check of his connection, asked for slack, and weighted the new system. With nearly full body weight on the tether and the carabiner locked, he told Mullen to take him off belay. After doing so, she walked around the formation to Nightstalker's base, where she began packing their gear.

Meanwhile, Parker untied from the rope and threaded it through the rappel anchors, then pulled the rope through the rings until both ends were on the ground. Approximately five minutes after taking her partner off belay, Mullen heard a yell and watched Parker fall from the top of the climb. He free-fell approximately 60 feet, then fell another 30 feet down lower-angled rock (70–80°) before hitting the ground.

Mullen found him lying on his back. His head was about one foot away from a small boulder. A trained Wilderness First Responder, Mullen stabilized Parker until a nearby climbing party arrived to help. The other climbers dialed 911 at 5 p.m. The climbers helped take vital signs and stabilize Parker until paramedics arrived at about 5:30 p.m. He was airlifted to Banner University Medical Center in Tucson.

Parker spent about three and a half weeks in the hospital and rehab center, with many broken bones, extensive abrasions, a mild traumatic brain injury, a nearly severed left ear, and nerve damage. After being discharged, Parker spent about two and a half months in a wheelchair and another month on crutches. Though still recovering, he was able to return to working on expedition and climbing courses in November 2021.

ANALYSIS

Due to some memory loss from the accident, the precise cause of the fall—and the five to ten minutes leading up to it—can only be hypothesized. Parker believes he initially clipped the end of his tether into the cordelette but that this connection was too long to give him easy access to the anchor. He must have tried to shorten his tether by clipping the second knotted loop of the sling.

After the accident, his locking carabiner remained clipped to the cordelette and locked shut. The tether was not compromised in any way. Parker assumes that when he tried to clip in, he pushed the knot through the opening of the locking carabiner but did not clip the actual loop of webbing. When he weighted the system, it is believed the knot jammed against the edge of the carabiner just enough to hold his weight. Parker's rappel device was still clipped to a gear loop on his harness after the fall. Likely the knot in the tether popped through the carabiner when his body weight shifted as he reached for the device.

Parker and Mullen recreated this scenario at home. They noted that while it was difficult to fully weight a knot placed in the carabiner this way, when it was set in a particular spot the knot could hold weight (especially when lodged in a smaller D-shaped locking carabiner). Once loaded, the jammed knot appeared similar to a properly clipped and loaded tether.

Many aspects of this accident line up with themes in other descending accidents. Since this was the last climb of the day, they felt pressure to depart for the two-hour drive back to Tucson. The couple were also about to start a three-week outdoor education course. Such transitions can be stressful and distracting. Parker reflected that the accident's primary cause was complacency, as he ultimately failed to catch his own mistake.

Other aspects are important as well. Parker had used his tether system many times, but more often for rappelling multi-pitch climbs. Using a new system—or an old system in a new context—raises a yellow flag that should be recognized. Perhaps the better option would have been to rig the system he used more commonly for cleaning bolted anchors on sport climbs. The only reason he used the system in question was because it was already rigged from his previous climb on Nightstalker.

Lastly, Parker was not wearing a helmet. This was a conscious decision. Before this accident, he regularly wore a helmet while leading and/or when concerned about overhead hazards. But since Naked Prey is a short, steep pitch on a small pinnacle of rock, rockfall was not an issue. As he was top-roping, there was little to no chance of hitting his head in a fall. Of all of the miracles herein, the greatest might be his avoidance of serious brain damage and/or death. Parker now wears his helmet in all outdoor roped climbing contexts. (*Sources: Tim Parker and Darcy Mullen.*)

The east side of Mt. Shasta in September 2012 (left) and September 2021 (right). Exceptionally dry conditions in 2021 contributed to a number of accidents on the mountain. *Phil Rhodes*

CALIFORNIA

BOULDER ROLLED ONTO LEG

Mt. Shasta, Clear Creek Route

On June 23, a lone male (31) was climbing the Clear Creek route. This moderate climb steepens to 3rd class near the "headwall" section at 13,000 feet. This portion scrambles through a relatively short section of steeper rock and talus to gain the summit area. The solo climber reported "accidentally pulling a 200-pound boulder onto his foot/ankle." He was unable to descend on his own and called 911.

U.S. Forest Service climbing ranger Nick Meyers was inserted by helicopter near 12,600 feet and ascended on foot to the injured climber's location. Meyers rigged the climber for evacuation, and California Highway Patrol Helicopter H-14 hoisted the patient to safety. The climber had torn ankle ligaments and suffered a knee injury.

ANALYSIS

The Clear Creek route is a strenuous 12-mile round trip with 7,800 feet of elevation gain. While nontechnical, the climb requires being attentive to usual mountain hazards, in this case large loose rocks. (*Source: Mt. Shasta Climbing Rangers.*)

Editor's Note: Mt. Shasta experienced an exceptionally dry and windy winter in 2020-21, leaving very little snow on the mountain by spring and possibly contributing to rockfall and loose-rock incidents. Perhaps fortunately, rangers issued fewer than half as many summit passes in 2021 as usual and conducted about half as many search and rescue missions.

FALLING ROCK

Mt. Shasta, Avalanche Gulch

In the afternoon of April 9, a solo climber took a glancing blow to the thigh by a quoted "500-pound rock" while climbing Avalanche Gulch. The climber was near the Heart, which is the steepest part of the route, with slopes reaching 35°.

Another solo climber nearby witnessed the incident and came to help. A 911 call was made, but after some reassessment, the injured was able to self-rescue with the aid of the other climber. The two scooted down the mountain to Helen Lake and then skied back to Bunny Flat. A large contusion was the reported extent of the injury.

ANALYSIS
Avalanche Gulch is technically the second-easiest route on Shasta, and the short approach makes it the most popular route to the summit (14,179 feet). Still, the 3rd-class difficulties and vertical gain of 7,300 feet add to the potential hazards one would expect from a big peak like this, including avalanches, altitude sickness, and rockfall. Getting a very early start is an essential strategy for minimizing some of these risks. (*Source: Mt. Shasta Climbing Rangers.*)

FALL ON SNOW | Unable to Self-Arrest
Mt. Shasta, Hotlum/Bolam Ridge

On June 19, a family of seven from Utah attempted to climb the Hotlum/Bolam Ridge route. By midmorning they had begun the steeper section of the route at 12,300 feet. They were all roped together—with no intermediate protection nor belay anchors—when one of them slipped and fell. The others were dragged off balance. Despite everyone's attempt to self-arrest, they were unable to stop until they all had fallen approximately 500 vertical feet. Miraculously, they came to rest just before hitting a boulder field.

A 17-year-old female suffered a broken tib/fib. The mother of the family sustained a crampon puncture to her calf but was able to self-rescue. Everyone else suffered minor injuries (cuts, abrasions, and contusions from sliding and tumbling on the rough, icy snow surfaces). Immediately after the fall, the family called 911. Climbing ranger Nick Meyers was inserted by California Highway Patrol Helicopter H-14, which quickly hoisted the female climber with the broken leg. The others self-rescued off the mountain.

ANALYSIS
The family stated they had moderate experience and had been practicing for the climb. Conditions on the route were icy, making self-arrest very difficult. This accident occurred at nearly the identical location of a fatality in September the year prior. Less than optimal conditions on Shasta can create problems for the under-equipped or uninitiated. The steep and often icy sections of this route require a level of awareness and experience somewhat higher than that possessed by novice visitors. (*Source: Mt. Shasta Climbing Rangers.*)

RAPPEL ERROR | Fracture, Spinal Injury
Northern Sierra, Rainbow

On May 27, while climbing at Rainbow, west of Donner Pass, I (Carl Alsup, 39) rappelled off the end of my rope. I had just led Malcolm's Route (5.9) to the top of the formation. My wife was going to follow but decided she was going to save her strength. So

I lowered, cleaned the route on top-rope, and then walked across the top of the cliff to the anchors of Aja (5.10d). I was still tied in. I clipped the rope through the two-bolt anchor, using slings to set up the top-rope. I threw one (unknotted) end of the rope down and saw it hit the ground. I then threw the other side of the rope, which was still attached to my harness so it formed a loop that didn't quite reach the ground.

I started to rappel and about 25 feet off the ground the free and unknotted rope end slipped through my device, and I fell into a pile of rocks and manzanita. My wife called for rescue, and despite being only a 15-minute walk from the road, the thick manzanita bushes necessitated a helicopter removal.

ANALYSIS
I've climbed outside for 20 years, trad for 19 years. From my own deconstruction, here's what happened: When I threw the side of the rope that was still tied to my harness, the weight of the rope pulled enough slack through the anchor to shorten the other end, so that it was 25 feet short of touching the ground. I failed to notice this shift at the anchor, and the free end of rope did not have a stopper knot so it slipped through the belay device when I rappelled. (*Source: Carl Alsup.*)

FALL ON ROCK | Inadequate Protection
Lake Tahoe Area, Cloudburst Canyon, Green Tongue Area

On July 17 my girlfriend, Hannah (29), and I (30) went out for a day in an obscure climbing area, just southeast of Lake Tahoe, called Cloudburst Canyon. On my third climb I fell at the crux, ripped three pieces of protection, and fell to the ground.

I have been climbing for six years with most of my experience on multi-pitch trad moderates. Ready to push the grades, train harder, and be okay with taking more falls on trad, I jumped right in and looked for some 5.11 trad routes. I had heard of Cloudburst Canyon from a new friend, Nate. He said the only beta was on Mountain Project. We looked and saw several classic climbs in the area, including a 5.11- for me to attempt. We arrived, met Nate, and headed into the canyon.

After a loose and technical approach, we warmed up on two routes, a 5.9 and then a 5.10-. Both felt solid, so I turned my eyes toward an obscure route called "Unknown 11-". I also saw a 10- directly to the right that shared anchors, which gave me the option of setting up a top-rope. I decided against this because of my new mindset. I was ready to lead harder climbs and was willing to fall. On the 11- route, the main feature was a lightning-bolt crack zigzagging up the slightly overhanging face. The first piece of protection was a bolt I could reach from the ground. After that it was going to be gear placements through the crux, then three bolts to the top.

A few moves into the climb, I placed a horizontal 0.3 Camalot in a shallow crack. Considering this route was at my limit, I didn't feel I had time to make sure it was perfect, so I moved on. After five more feet, the gear was getting harder to place. I placed a small offset nut that passed a few tugs and looked decent. I kept climbing. I reached a bit of a rest and got another small offset nut above my head. I fired into the crux and got about five or six feet above my last piece when I couldn't move up safely anymore. I did not want to come off desperately reaching for holds, so I yelled "Falling!" as I let go of the wall. I felt tension in the rope and then a "SNAP!" The next thing

Below the crux on Unknown 5.11-. *Kyle Broxterman*

I knew I was on the ground, about 15 feet downhill from the start of the route. I'd fallen about 30 feet to the ground. The only thing keeping me from continuing down was Nate arresting my fall through the only piece left in the wall–the bolt at the start.

I had landed standing up, shattering my right calcaneus and fully fracturing the talus bone in my left foot. We quickly realized that getting me out of this remote canyon alone was not realistic. Nate went looking for some climbers we had spotted on the way up.

With Hannah holding my right leg up, I started slowly sliding and crawling down the loose slope. Nate came back with three other climbers. As a team of four, they slowly moved me down the talus, loose rock, ledges, stream crossings, and stinging nettles. The full effort took three hours. I made it to urgent care and had surgery two weeks later.

ANALYSIS

I made three placements that failed on this climb. The highest was a number 2 or 3 DMM Peenut offfset (rated to 5kN), whose wire broke, leaving the head of the nut still stuck in the rock. Next down was another offset (a number 1 DMM Peenut) that ripped out of the wall, followed by a number 0.3 Camalot.

The first lesson was to understand the limits of my gear. A microwire rated to 5kN could handle a short fall under perfect circumstances, but I was too close to the ground with little slack in the rope. I essentially shock-loaded this wire and broke it. I learned to pay attention to the entire system and how each part plays a different role in the forces applied to my pieces of protection. Second, as a heavier climber (around 200 lbs.), I need to start taking fall ratings on gear more seriously. If I am placed in a situation where small gear is required, I should be nesting and/or placing them frequently instead of relying on one small piece every six feet. The third is to get the best placement possible. If you have doubts, don't just move past it in the hopes that it will hold. If you can't find good protection, consider lowering or aid climbing.

The main lesson I learned was to approach climbing with a more focused and safety-oriented attitude. Over the last six years, I had numbed that sense of caution by climbing mostly within my onsight ability. Because I was not taking any falls, I slowly built up a false sense of security both in the gear I was placing and my climbing abilities. This laissez-faire attitude was the reason I skipped many safety checks that day, which could have made this accident possibly fatal.

Considering all the following mistakes I made, I feel extremely lucky with how the accident turned out:

(1) I skipped the opportunity to climb a much easier route and set up a top-rope in order to get gear and movement beta for a route that was at my onsight limit.

(2) I was in a new climbing area and did not consider the rock quality. I found out after the fact that the granite in this area and the specific climb was known to be crumbly at the surface.

(3) I chose to fall instead of simply downclimbing to my piece and resting. If I had done this, the piece would most likely have held and I could have reassessed.

(4) I chose not to wear a helmet. I had convinced myself the situation didn't call for it: no climbers above, not a multi-pitch climb, and I chose comfort over safety.

(5) None of us had a first aid kit, which would have been critical had my injuries been worse. (*Source: Kyle Broxterman.*)

SLIP ON THIRD-CLASS TRAVERSE
Tahoe Area, Newly Developed Area

I (Bobby Hutton, 31) wanted to show my friend Adam a new area that my friends and I were developing. In early April, we decided to drop lines down a cliff to work on new routes.

To access the top of the cliff, we crossed a steep granite gully and gained about a hundred feet of elevation on easier terrain on the left side of the gully. We started to cross back on the third-class terrain above the gully to access the top of the cliff. I then slipped in such I way that I was able to grab the rock but not stop myself. I tumbled down over 100 feet. I remember multiple impacts on my feet and one on my head, which knocked off my helmet. (*Editor's Note: Hutton's helmet was unbuckled at the time. See below.*)

Adam scrambled down to where I stopped falling. He called 911 and supported me as I crawled to a flat bench in the granite. Once the paramedics arrived, they decided to have a California Highway Patrol helicopter long-line me out and deliver me to an ambulance down the hill. After X-rays and CT scans at the local hospital, I was transferred to UC Davis Medical Center. I spent four days in the hospital during which they operated on my thumb and ankle.

A Tahoe-area climber fell 100 feet after slipping off the top of a new crag. *Bobby Hutton*

ANALYSIS

If you take over a million steps in 3rd- or 4th-class terrain, you are going to slip a few times. This slip just wasn't recoverable. I do not feel complacency was an issue. I was very aware of the risks, having had and seen several near misses in the last ten years. I am extremely happy that I decided to put my helmet on my head for the approach up the hill instead if clipping it to my harness or putting it in my backpack. It was a tight, uncomfortable fit due to my large head and thick hair. Even unclipped, I still credit it as saving me from brain injury or death. My WFR training allowed me to stay calm and effectively communicate with EMS personnel. It was a tiny investment for the peace of mind it brought me during the accident. (*Source: Bobby Hutton.*)

FALL ON ROCK | Off Route, Inadequate Protection
Yosemite National Park, Five Open Books

On March 4, two climbers, "Jeff" and "Erin," climbed Munginella (3 pitches, 5.6) to the base of Selaginella (4 pitches, 5.8) in the Five Open Books area near Yosemite Falls. The pair were both experienced, and these routes were within their ability. Erin led all the pitches on Munginella, and Jeff, the more experienced traditional climber of the two, proceeded to lead all the pitches on Selaginella.

On the final pitch, Jeff was attempting to move quickly and place gear in such a manner to make it easier for Erin, as she was uncharacteristically struggling that day. Near the top of the pitch, Jeff became disoriented above a run-out slab. He ended up on a small ledge and placed a single 0.4 Black Diamond cam that he felt was questionable. Jeff thought the topo had shown the route continuing left. When he looked in that direction, he saw something that resembled a Mountain Project photo that said: "not the way to end the climb." He also remembered verbiage about an alternate "flake" finish. Jeff and Erin could not see nor hear each other due to the meandering route and noise from the waterfall.

Jeff began climbing delicate right-angling flakes, unable to get protection but finding the climbing easy. Approximately 15 feet above the ledge, Jeff started searching for protection, as he only had the questionable 0.4 cam below. He remembered the route description saying that just below the anchor protection was sparse, so he believed he was on route.

The Five Open Books link-up of (A) Munginella and (B) Selaginella. The walk-off is to the left. *NPS Image*

Jeff became nervous and contemplated downclimbing but continued another 15 feet to a slab. The slab did not match any route description and so, with his last piece of protection 25 to 30 feet below him, Jeff decided to downclimb back to the ledge. During the downclimb, a flake pulled off as he tested it. Jeff lost his balance and fell. He believes he struck the ledge and continued falling for a total of 50 feet. The 0.4 cam caught him.

Remarkably, Jeff was able to finish the climb, despite a right ankle fracture and severe bone bruising in the left heel. After bringing up his partner, they contacted Yosemite Search and Rescue (YOSAR) to get help with the hike down the Yosemite Falls Trail. Their ability to make it to the top of the climb greatly expedited the rescue response time and limited the risk for the SAR team.

ANALYSIS

Mountain Project is a useful tool, but it has plenty of information that can be misleading or incorrect. Published topos are often more reliable and objective. Jeff remarked that the overload of information on the site made it more difficult to remember accurate information during the climb.

Carrying beta with you on the route is ideal, so you can refer to it as needed and not rely on memory. Take photos of guidebooks/topos. If you can cut through the overload of information, download the Mountain Project app. (*Source: Yosemite National Park Climbing Rangers.*)

STRANDED | Exposure and Weather
Yosemite National Park, Half Dome

In the evening of October 17, two climbers, Kate (28) and Nick (26), started up the Regular Northwest Face of Half Dome (23 pitches, 5.9 C2) after completing the Nose on El Capitan (31 pitches, 5.9 C2) earlier in the same day. Nick and Kate were both experienced climbers attempting a sub-24-hour link-up of the two walls. They failed to summit Half Dome when they were caught in a winter storm, five pitches from the top.

After finishing The Nose, Kate and Nick ate lunch and started up the approach to Half Dome. The weather forecasted a 90 percent chance of precipitation around 1:30 a.m. Despite that, neither talked about rescheduling.

Kate and Nick started climbing the Northwest Face around 6 p.m. They made good progress, but around midnight they were engulfed in a winter-like storm. At this point, Nick and Kate were simul-climbing through 5.9 and 5.10 terrain, with snow and ice accumulating on ledges and in cracks. Around 12:30 a.m., they arrived at Big Sandy Ledge, atop pitch 18.

Nick began leading the first pitch of the "Zig Zags" (pitch 19) with increasing difficulty. He was scraping ice out of the cracks and, at one point, slipped off a large foot ledge and fell back onto his daisy chain. Their gear was freezing solid, and Kate's hands were losing their ability to function.

Nick still wanted to try and summit, but Kate did not think safely continuing was possible. At this point, they had not sustained any injuries, but the pitches ahead included Thank God Ledge and multiple slab pitches, none of which is inconsequential, especially if covered with ice and snow. They called 911 at 1:50 a.m. and were told

Nick and Kate being hoisted to the summit of Half Dome after a mid-October storm. Big Sandy and Thank God ledges are clearly outlined below by the plastering of fresh snow. *Jack Cramer*

to call back at 6 a.m. In a few hours the snow stopped falling, the wind died down, and the temperature dropped. At first light, the conditions on the route were even icier. At 6 a.m., they called search and rescue back and confirmed they needed assistance.

Shortly afterward, Yosemite Search and Rescue (YOSAR) gathered for a technical rescue on Half Dome. The plan was to fly rescuers, ropes, and all necessary equipment to the summit with a helicopter and lower one member of YOSAR to Nick and Kate and then haul them up to the summit. Due to the cold winter conditions, the helicopter got delayed because the rotors needed to de-ice.

Later that morning, conditions allowed the helicopter to fly. A rescuer was lowered to Nick and Kate, carrying jackets and warm beverages. Once the rescuer attached to Kate and Nick, two teams on top raised the climbers to the summit. Miraculously, neither Kate nor Nick sustained any cold-related injuries.

ANALYSIS

Heed the forecast. Severe storms can roll through Yosemite any month of the year, but early spring and late fall often catch climbers unaware. In this case, the team saw a forecast for the Valley floor (4,000 feet elevation) with precipitation starting at 1:30 a.m., and they were surprised when the storm started two hours earlier. The conditions on Half Dome (8,846 feet) were not surprisingly much more intense and severe.

Don't allow the goal to blind your judgment. The link-up of Half Dome and El Capitan in under 24 hours is an admirable goal for any Valley climber. After a season of training and a plan set in motion, it can be tough to decide to bail, especially given that the climbers had completed El Capitan and were "on track" for a sub-24-hour time. They ignored a known weather risk to complete their goal.

Communicate openly with your partner. Many accidents and rescues can be avoided with better communication between partners. Any reservations or concerns should be immediately communicated. Especially with disappointment on the line, it can be challenging to start the conversation. Partners, particularly new partners, should regularly check in and practice their communication like other climbing skills. Sure, one partner might be disappointed at first, but if it means not having to spend the night in a winter storm or worse, it might be worth it.

Although they discussed the weather, there was no conversation about a worst-case scenario. The climbers didn't discuss the possibility of not making it to the top nor what the upper pitches would be like in a storm. The final pitch of the Regular Northwest Face is slab climbing with limited opportunities to aid. There should always be a conversation about how to retreat if there is no real possibility of going up.

Pack the proper layers. If you know there is a chance of precipitation, you should pack suitable layers. Kate and Nick both had warm gloves (Kate was not initially wearing them), base layers, and hardshell jackets. However, neither had hardshell pants, and they felt like that was a major mistake. Both Kate and Nick have experience with ice/mixed climbing in winter conditions and thought they could have possibly self-rescued the following morning with the appropriate layers.

Know when to call for a rescue (and have the ability to communicate). It's tough to know when the right time is. Ultimately, Kate decided they should call for help when she felt like she could not safely use her hands. The need for a rescue became more apparent when they were rappelling back down to Big Sandy after attempting the Zig-Zags. The ropes were extremely icy, making the rappel dangerous. They rappelled with Grigris and used slings as "third-hand" backup prusiks, and did not feel it was safe to try and retreat further. There were legitimate concerns that if they attempted to continue upward, Kate and/or Nick could have gotten injured; this would have made the situation much worse and the rescue more complex.

They only carried one cell phone with them, and fortunately they were able to make a phone call to 911. To communicate with YOSAR, they kept the phone off when not in use and kept the phone next to their bodies to keep it warm and preserve the battery. (*Source: Yosemite National Park Climbing Rangers.*)

FALL ON ROCK | Roped Soloing, Inadequate Protection
Yosemite National Park, Manure Pile Buttress

On April 13, Yosemite Search and Rescue (YOSAR) responded to a roped soloist who had fallen and injured himself while climbing the second pitch of After Six (5 pitches, 5.7) on Manure Pile Buttress. It was reported that the rope-soloist had come to Yosemite originally intending to climb with a partner. He was an experienced climber in his mid-50s and, unable to find a partner, he decided to rope-solo this relatively easy route.

The soloist initially scrambled up a 3rd-class ledge to the right of the first pitch. From there, he set his first anchor and began to rope-solo, belaying himself as he climbed. It is unclear precisely what self-belay system he was using. While climbing the second pitch he fell, taking a large pendulum swing and hitting the wall,

injuring his neck. He attempted to self-rescue and lower himself to the ground but was in too much pain. He called Yosemite Search and Rescue to assist in the rescue.

Within one hour of the incident, YOSAR arrived. A team member scrambled up 3rd class to the base of the second pitch—the location of the injured climber. Rescuers built an anchor and packaged the patient in a litter, then lowered a rescuer and patient to the ground, where he was carried out in a wheeled litter to El Capitan Picnic Area.

ANALYSIS

In this case, placing extra gear may have lessened the length and severity of the fall. In low-angle terrain (often found on "easy" climbs in the 5.6–5.8 range), a leader fall of almost any length can result in hitting a ledge, causing injury. Additionally, the risk of a head or neck injury is greatly increased in low-angle terrain, where a backward fall could flip

Manure Pile Buttress. A rescuer being lowered to the ground with the patient in a litter. *NPS Photo*

the climber upside down before hitting the rock. This climber was wearing a helmet.

Climbing with a partner is usually safer. Having another uninjured person to help in the case of an accident could be the difference between being able to self-rescue or needing to call search and rescue. In this case, luckily, the climber had cell phone service. Be sure to know when and where you may have reception in case of an emergency. (*Source: Yosemite National Park Climbing Rangers.*)

FALL ON ROCK | Free Soloing
Yosemite National Park, Manure Pile Buttress

On April 11, Josh Ourada (31) fell while free soloing Nutcracker (5 pitches, 5.8) on the Manure Pile Buttress. Ourada has been climbing for over ten years and was no stranger to free soloing. He had climbed Nutcracker before, both with and without a rope.

Ourada was halfway up pitch four, climbing over a bulge with poor feet, when his foot, hand, or both slipped. He fell 150 to 200 feet to a ledge. From his recollection, his back was to the wall during the fall. He was using his feet, hands, and body to try and slow the descent. Ourada landed, seated on a boulder, at the belay ledge for the start of pitch three. A climber on the belay ledge had to jump out of the way.

Climbers in the area heard screams followed by the thud of Ourada landing in the ledge. 911 was called. The climber who had dodged Ourada stayed with him for several hours until a helicopter rescue was completed. Ourada's injuries included a shattered right heel, fractured pelvis, lacerated left foot, several broken ribs, collapsed lung, and a severely injured L1 vertebra (burst fracture). He also had significant road rash.

ANALYSIS
Free soloing is inherently dangerous, with little room for error, even for the most talented and experienced soloists. Ourada had retreated on free solo climbs before if he felt any deficits. This time, in hindsight, Ourada thinks he might not have been in the right headspace.

It's assumed that a free solo climber is taking their life into their own hands. However, consideration must be given to other climbers who might be affected and to the safety of the rescuers. Neither bystanders nor SAR members have signed on to the soloist's risky interpretation of the game. Ourada is remorseful for putting other climbers and rescue personnel in harm's way. (*Sources: Josh Ourada, Climbing Magazine, and the Editors.*)

FALLING ROCK
Yosemite National Park, El Capitan

On June 16, Matthew "Mash" Alexander (50) was struck by rockfall in the face and head as he slept. He and his climbing partner, Sean McGinness (48), were bivying in hammocks midway up El Cap, near the Nose route.

The team had spent seven nights on the wall while climbing Triple Direct (VI 5.9 C2). This route joins the upper third of The Nose (a very popular route in June), and they had chosen to retreat to avoid crowding with other teams. Alexander had climbed El Cap 43 times before. McGinness was on his first Yosemite big wall.

While retreating, the team got off the standard rappel route and found themselves on an aid route called Grape Race (5.9 A3). On their eighth night on the wall, the pair set up their hammocks bunk-bed-style and bivyed. According to *Climbing* magazine Alexander said, "I had a night of tossing and turning. I also had the feeling we were in the flight pattern of stuff that could get dropped from above."

In the early morning, rockfall struck. Alexander was hit by a fist-size rock in the head and face, rupturing his eye and exposing his brain. McGinness, who was sleeping on the lower level, heard the rock strike Alexander. He moved to respond and his hammock, also damaged by the rockfall, collapsed, sending him on a body-length fall. His backup caught him, and he was able to help his friend and call SAR via cell phone.

In around three hours, Yosemite Search and Rescue arrived and Alexander was flown off the wall, followed by McGinness. At UC Davis Medical Center, Alexander had the first of three surgeries to rebuild his skull and install a prosthetic eye.

ANALYSIS
Natural rockfall, human-generated rocks, and dropped gear are all too common on this and other Yosemite big walls. *Climbing* magazine reported that Alexander is uncertain whether another team accidentally dislodged the rocks or if it was a random act of nature. He says it doesn't matter. "To me, getting hit, it was just something that happened." While sleeping, McGinness was wearing a helmet, but Alexander was not. He says he would do so in the future. (*Sources: Climbing.com and the Editors.*)

FALL ON ROCK | Inadequate Projection, Inexperience
Yosemite National Park, Cathedral Peak

On August 13, BJ Cook and I responded to an accident while climbing on the Southeast Buttress of Cathedral Peak, a five-pitch, 5.6 traditional climb in Tuolumne Meadows. BJ and I are experienced climbers and have many moderate multi-pitch trad climbs under our belt.

At approximately 8:30 a.m., we began the route and completed two pitches, ending at a small pine tree. Below and to the right, two young women were climbing a different variation.

A few minutes later, we heard a loud, heavy sound of impact from below. We saw the leader falling on the low-angle slab until her belayer, located on a small ledge, arrested the fall. The leader had fallen over 30 feet, hitting a large ledge before rolling down the slabs.

We called down and asked if they were okay. Neither the belayer nor the leader acknowledged us, and the leader appeared unconscious. For a few moments, we continued to call down to the party below, and the leader began to moan, then scream, so we decided to call 911. After BJ called for a rescue, he lowered me. The leader's fall had been held by a number 1 Camalot in a small alcove. There was an additional piece below. The belayer was holding the leader's weight via an ATC belay device, and the leader was laid out on a low-angle slab, unable to support her weight or aid in her own rescue.

Rescue on Cathedral Peak. *NPS Photo*

We did not have enough rope to double-rope rappel to them, so I rappeled as far as their number 1 Camalot and incorporated this into an anchor. BJ then rappelled to this station, and I then rappelled on two ropes to the injured party and the belayer. The belayer had tied a catastrophe knot behind the ATC. She was not tied into an anchor but was sitting behind a tree on the small ledge. After the fall, she looped a section of her rope around a tree and clove-hitched it to a non-locking carabiner on her belay loop.

I went to the injured climber. She was in and out of consciousness over the next few minutes, hanging in her harness, and in great pain. I continued rappelling to the belayer and we tied off her device with a mule hitch so she could go hands-free. I then made an anchor by slinging the tree and tethered her with a sling and locking carabiner.

I returned to the injured climber and supported her while the belayer slowly lowered the climber. We were eventually able to get the injured climber to a safe and comfortable position on the ledge. We then waited for the rescue team. A different group of climbers retrieved all the gear, and I moved out of the way while SAR did their job. The injured leader was hoisted off the ledge in a litter and taken to Fresno. We helped the belayer rappel to the base, and she hiked out with SAR.

ANALYSIS
The party's rack consisted of fewer than ten pieces: a few nuts and Tricams and three or four Camalots, which they had borrowed from a friend. The party carried no alpine draws, only quickdraws.

Failure to adequately protect the route—which is common on easier terrain—likely contributed to the injuries sustained during the fall. However, their limited gear and lack of proper belay anchor suggest that they would have benefited from some additional education and experience. (*Source: Matthew Lee.*)

FALL ON 4TH-CLASS ROCK | Climbing Unroped
High Sierra, Palisades

On May 31, Vik Waghray (24) fell to his death while traversing from Temple Crag to Mt. Gayley. He and Michael Layton (45) were attempting the long and arduous Temple-Gayley-Sill-Thunderbolt traverse.

The pair had summited Temple Crag and were on their way to Gayley. While scrambling unroped on 4th-class terrain, Layton, concerned about the loose rock, warned Waghray to maintain three points of contact. Shortly after this, Waghray either slipped or dislodged a rock, falling 2,000 feet to his death.

ANALYSIS
While climbing unroped comes with its own set of risks, it is a huge time saver and a necessary technique to succeed on long alpine routes. Doing so entails extra focus over an extended period of time. Layton, a veteran of many long routes in the High Sierra, cautions climbers against trusting guidebooks or other climbers' trip reports too much, as he contends that such resources don't convey the danger and looseness of the terrain. In 2014, a solo climber from Chicago was found dead after attempting the Temple-Gayley-Thunderbolt traverse. (*Source: Michael Layton.*)

GROUND FALL | Rappel Error
Echo Cliffs, The Grotto

My wife (Kelly Perkins, 59) and I (Craig Perkins, 60) have rock climbed for 20 years. After a long hiatus, I took time to refresh my skills, including anchor building, knots, and gear placement. Our climb, Miss Pacman (5.9, sport), was fun and initially uneventful. Upon reaching the top of the 40-foot route, the open cold-shuts anchors looked worn. Over the years, deep grooves had formed in the metal. I attached two quickdraws to facilitate top-roping, one to each shut and clipped the rope-bearing end with the carabiner gates opposite and opposing. This minimized wear and tear on the shuts.

I decided to rappel from the anchors instead of lowering through the shuts. To secure myself, I attached two quickdraws to my belay loop and clipped one to each shut. Once secure, I gave the command, "Off belay." Still tied in, I unclipped the rope from the hanging quickdraws and looped it through the open shuts to set up a rappel.

I then girth-hitched a Dyneema sling to my belay loop and tied a figure eight on a bight in the sling (Mistake #1). I slid the end loop over both open shuts (Mistake #2). The loop formed by the figure eight was so small that it created a wide angle in the loop (Mistake #3). I did not set up my rappel system before committing myself to the sling, nor did I test the sling while belayed or backed up by my anchor quick-draws (Mistake #4).

I cleaned the anchor quickdraws and sat back on the Dyneema sling. As I did so, the loop constricted and popped off the open cold shuts. I began falling. My first reaction was to grab the opposite side of the rope. While this slowed my descent, it also caused a friction burn. I instinctively let go, only to grab the rope again as I picked up speed. The rope burn caused me to let go again and I continued to the ground, landing on a flat slab at the base of the climb. Fortunately, my injuries were limited to third-degree burns on all fingers of the right hand and two fingers on the left, along with a sprained ankle, scrapes on my back, and a hematoma to my left thigh. I was very lucky.

My wife and I gathered our belongings and returned to the trailhead after a one-hour hike. We headed straight to the closest urgent care center, where my hands were treated. Suffice to say, this was a lesson learned. I hope this story will help prevent further accidents of this kind. The event scared the bejesus out of my wife. She initially thought she had made a mistake by taking me off belay. To be clear, she did nothing wrong. Also, she was a trooper by carrying extra weight during our hike out. (*Source: Craig Perkins.*)

ANALYSIS
Open cold shuts are thankfully disappearing as anchor hardware gets updated. Unfortunately, they are still found even on popular climbs. This incident illustrates two major hazards presented by open cold shuts. First, rope wear on the anchor reduces their already low relative strength. The second is they are inherently insecure, just like any open anchor.

The victim noted that during years of repeated lowering, "deep grooves had formed" in the shuts. Though he made a good choice to top-rope through quickdraws, a better option would have been to girth-hitch two independent slings (or the two ends of one long sling) to the shuts and equalize the rope-bearing end.

The biggest lesson here is to weight-test the system (in this case the rappel) before unclipping from your direct tether to the anchor. A decision to rappel versus lower is a personal choice. In this case, the complexity of reconfiguring an open anchor was inefficient and paradoxically precipitated what might have become a fatal accident. The victim's desire to create "extra redundant protection" was also unnecessary and, again, exposed him to more risk. In the end, it would have been easier and safer to lower through the cold shuts, grooved as they were. (*Source: The Editors.*)

ROCKFALL

High Desert, Apple Valley Area, Alessandria

On Saturday, March 6, Tylea Brown (39) and her husband, Casey Cruz (32), accompanied by their two young daughters, were enjoying climbing in the Southern California high desert. After completing several single-pitch routes, Brown was belaying Cruz on top-rope. As Cruz climbed, he noticed small, spontaneous rockfall to the side of the route. He peered above, over a ledge, and saw a rock about the size of two microwave ovens begin to fall. His right hand was in a crack as he shouted "ROCK!" Cruz then attempted to shift the rock's course with his left hand, but it was too heavy. He did manage to push away a smaller rock that followed.

On the ground, Brown shifted her body in an attempt to shield her daughters and avoid the falling boulder. Despite this, the

Tylea Brown and the boulder that claimed her leg. *Casey Cruz*

rock crashed onto Brown, crushing her left leg. Brown was belaying with an Edelrid Jul 2—a single-rope belay device with some assisted-braking capability. This helped keep Cruz safe as he witnessed the collision and severe injury. As Cruz quickly rigged his rappel, Brown pulled her nearly detached foot out from under the boulder and held it above her head. Her shoe remained under the rock. Cruz arrived at Brown's side and tied a tourniquet above her ankle and stabilized her foot with an ACE bandage.

Concerned about the possibility of bleeding out, Brown hopped and then scooted down the steep quarter-mile trail to their truck, with Cruz's assistance. They then drove to meet the incoming ambulance. First responders continued to stabilize Brown until a helicopter arrived to airlift her to Loma Linda trauma center.

The next day, Cruz returned to the scene and cleared other loose rocks from the route. He later learned that three small earthquakes had struck the area on the day of the accident. These seismic events might have shifted the rocks.

Brown has required multiple surgeries, including a below-the-knee amputation. As she continues the long path of healing, she has been fitted with a prosthetic, allowing a return to a number of outdoor sports. She hopes to climb again in the future.

ANALYSIS
Rockfall is a risk in all types of climbing. Cruz and Brown did many things that contributed to lessening injury to both of them. Cruz's awareness of his surroundings and prompt verbal warning gave Brown just enough time to partially protect herself and her children. The use of an assisted-braking device kept Cruz safe while on belay. Having the right equipment on his harness allowed Cruz to self-rescue and rappel. Their medical equipment and first-aid knowledge helped stabilize Brown's injuries. Finally, the team maintained a sense of composure and demonstrated phenomenal grit on the descent to their truck. This shortened the interval between accident and definitive care. (*Sources: Tylea Brown and the Editors.*)

BOULDERING FALL
Joshua Tree National Park, Echo Rock Boulders

In March, Lucy Kim (23) fell from Classic Thin Crack (V2) in Joshua Tree, severely damaging her left ankle. With her hands at the top, Kim chose to jump off in order to retry the problem. Below were six crash pads and two spotters. She fell in an upright posture but impacted with her left foot turned inward and the pad was curved over a rock. A spotter prevented her from falling backward, but the torque turned her foot even more inward as the spotter pushed her forward.

Kim was driven to the hospital with an open ankle dislocation and torn ligaments, tendons, and nerves. She is making a full recovery and has resumed climbing, though she still hadn't regained full range of motion a year after the accident.

ANALYSIS
In bouldering, every fall is a ground fall. Kim notes, "I should've looked down to spot my landing before jumping, but I was instead looking at my next hold." Be aware of an uneven landing. "The lesson would be to check the landing (what the ground actually looks like beneath pads), and to always be conscious of how and where you're landing." (*Source: Lucy Kim.*)

LEG STUCK IN CRACK
Joshua Tree National Park, Left Horse Area

On a spring day in Joshua Tree, a climber returned to practice roped soloing after many years away from the sport. He started up Granny Goose (5.7), a 50-foot traditional route in a well-traveled area. After passing the initial flake on the route, he placed his leg into an offwidth crack, about 30 feet above the ground.

Fairly quickly, the climber realized his left leg was stuck. He was well positioned with a cam overhead and an edge for his right foot, and a rock inside the crack allowed him to push off with the left foot, but he still had no luck in releasing the leg. Swelling developed, making the situation more concerning.

Since bathroom facilities were nearby, the climber was able to call down to other visitors. He stayed as calm as possible and asked for rangers to be contacted. He then lowered a bight of rope for those below to attach a bottle of water and then a pocket knife that he had at the base in his pack. He considered their suggestion of lubricating his leg with sunscreen but was concerned the slippery sunscreen would endanger future climbers on the route. Ultimately, the climber was able to extricate his limb after cutting the leg off his pants and was able to descend safely.

ANALYSIS

Many climbers have experienced the panicked feeling of having a limb become stuck on a climb. These usually can be freed by shuffling the foot or removing the shoe. This climber managed to stay calm while troubleshooting. He was also well positioned, with people available nearby to assist him. Other techniques previously used to free stuck limbs include creating anchor systems to lift the weight off the affected limb and using lubricants such as dish soap. (*Sources: Mountain Project and the Editors.*)

BOULDERING FALL | Insufficient Pad Placement
San Diego, Santee Boulders

On the afternoon of March 6, Joseph Chen (33) fell from near the top of American Express (5.9). The climb is described on Mountain Project as a top-rope. However, the 15-foot granite slab is often climbed as a boulder problem. Chen was unroped.

Chen wrote, "The group I was with was highballing this climb. I was not familiar with the area, and it seemed higher than something I would normally boulder. I tried two times but bailed halfway up. I tried one more time as my last climb of the day and pushed beyond where I would normally feel comfortable. I had relatively good feet but somehow lost my footing while searching for the last hold."

Chen fell down the slab, landing directly on his heels on a single crash pad placed among a scattering of other pads. He was evacuated by two other climbers and driven to urgent care. X-rays revealed a severe burst compression fracture of the L1 vertebra that necessitated a complete replacement of the vertebra with a cage, along with fusion of the T11 to L3 vertebrae to stabilize his spine. The trauma doctor was surprised that he was able to self-rescue and considered Chen very lucky to have escaped paralysis.

ANALYSIS

Bouldering is dangerous. Chen spent the next seven months in bed for most of the day. He started climbing again but at a much lower level due to loss of flexibility and strength.

Chen says in hindsight that one crash pad was insufficient, and he should have personally repositioned the multiple pads rather than relying on placement by others. He also would do his own research instead of going with the will of the group; he noted that he wouldn't have attempted the route as a highball had he known it was considered a top-rope. Finally, his spotters failed him. They were inattentive, and he noted that some had started drinking. (*Source: Joseph Chen.*)

COLORADO

FALL ON ICE | Inadequate Protection
Telluride, Bridalveil Falls

On February 1, Michael Levy (31) suffered a broken fibula after taking a leader fall on the second pitch of Bridalveil Falls (3 pitches, WI5+) near Telluride. He and climbing partner Tom Bohanon (65) effected a self-rescue to the nearby access road before being transported by local SAR to their vehicle. Below is Levy's edited report:

We arrived at the trailhead at 3:45 a.m. The approach took approximately 1 hour 30 minutes. We left our skis below the snow-covered talus slope leading up to the climb. It was twilight when we began racking up, and it was still difficult to see much beyond the glow of our headlamps.

The first pitch was extremely wet, and the ice was poor quality. I made most of my upward progress by hooking my tools behind ice petals. I occasionally yelled down to Bo (who had climbed the route on six prior occasions) to ask which way I should go. Sixty meters up, I reached a sheltered ice cave and made an anchor with two ice screws in solid blue ice. I brought Bo up.

After sipping some tea and restacking the rope, I prepared to set off on pitch two. We had brought 15 ice screws, and I wanted as many of them as possible for the next 60-meter lead. Therefore, I removed the shorter of the two screws from the anchor, leaving the bomber 21cm screw. [*The reconfigured anchor included Bohanon's two ice tools, planted above the single screw, all equalized with a cordelette, with the power point one foot below the screw. After a failed initial attempt on the next pitch, Levy retreated. He then chose a direct path toward the next belay.*]

Not wanting to sacrifice any of my 14 screws, I decided against putting in a first screw as I normally would a short distance after leaving the belay. Two meters above the belay, a blob of ice beneath my left foot disintegrated. Both tools popped from their hook placements, and I fell approximately five meters. [*This was a factor-two fall, past his belayer.*]

My right foot was bent against the inside of my calf, the sole of my boot facing upward. Bo had been sucked up

View from the litter. Bridalveil Falls in the background. *Michael Levy*

into the anchor. We decided the best course of action would be for Bo to lower me to the ground with his Grigri and then rappel from a V-thread. I removed my right crampon so that it wouldn't catch on the ice as I lowered.

When I got to the ground, I butt-scooted to our packs. I called San Miguel County Search and Rescue. They explained that if I could get to my skis (500 feet below) on the access road, the rescue would be straightforward.

I crawled and butt-scooted to the road while Bo rigged his rappel. SAR arrived 45 minutes later with snowmobiles and a litter. Once back at the trailhead, Bo and I drove to Telluride Medical Center, where the doctor confirmed a broken fibula.

ANALYSIS

Given a WI5+ grade, Bridalveil was at the time in extra challenging conditions. Levy believes his accident was the combination of several bad decisions and bad luck.

First, the ice was in poor condition, triggering the fall. Second, the scale of the route and its maze of ice daggers, cauliflowers, and mushrooms led to route-finding difficulties and the choice of the ill-fated line.

He also failed to place adequate protection when it was readily available. There are two situations while leading water ice when it is essential to stop and place an ice screw. One is very soon after leaving the belay, and the other is prior to clearing a bulge.

Levy's decision to forgo placing a screw above the anchor was, in his own words, "foolish." The factor-two fall onto a one-screw anchor (ice axes are inadequate as anchors) could have been easily avoided. "I knew I should place a screw above the belay but was intent on conserving my supply. Thankfully the anchor held up, but it was an unnecessary risk." (*Sources: Michael Levy and Tom Bohanon.*)

RAPPEL ERROR | Inadequate Knot Block
Ouray, Camp Bird Road

On January 29, veteran climbers Tom Bohanon (65) and Wayne McIlwraith (74) experienced a rappelling accident while descending from Chockstone Chimney (WI3) in the Camp Bird Road area. Injuries were thankfully minor.

Bohanon and McIlwraith climbed Chockstone Chimney (WI3-4) in a single long pitch. They descended via rappel using a single 9.2mm by 70m rope paired with a 6mm static retrieval line of the same length. The anchor was webbing with a stainless-steel rappel ring and carabiner at the power point. The two ropes were joined by an overhand knot (a.k.a. offset overhand bend) jammed against the rappel ring and carabiner. This technique, known as a "knot block," prevents the rope from sliding through the rappel ring and carabiner in one direction but allows it to slide through the

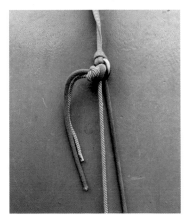

Example of an overhand rigged as a knot block at a rappel ring. Once down, the climbers would pull the thinner yellow rope.

other direction. This would facilitate a rappel of the single 9.2mm while allowing the team to retrieve the ropes.

The retrieval line was backed up by a figure 8 knot clipped to the anchor. Bohanon rappelled without incident, using a Grigri on the single 9.2mm. He stopped on the snow slope at the base of the climb (about ten feet above flat terrain). McIlwraith saw no movement in the jammed knot. After Bohanon reached the base, McIlwraith untied the backup and then duplicated the rappel on the single 9.2mm. Meanwhile, on the snow slope, Bohanon clipped the retrieval line to his harness with two feet of slack to act as a backup. He also held the single 9.2mm in a fireman's belay. McIlwraith rappelled uneventfully and passed Bohanon, who by necessity released the fireman's belay. When he was three feet above flat ground, the knot at the anchor popped through the power point and McIlwraith fell backward. He landed on his back upon a 20° snow slope. The retrieval line came tight on Bohanon's harness just as his partner's fall/slide ended. McIlwraith experienced a sore back and neck. His symptoms dissipated after a few days.

ANALYSIS

While the injuries were minor, the accident illustrates that the most experienced climbers, using tried and true methods, must be ever vigilant on a descent.

More than one accident last year involved the failure of a jammed knot, whether deliberate or unintentional (*see page 24*). Given the myriad types and sizes of carabiners, rings, links, hooks, and hangers at anchors, a single strategy won't address all situations. Fortunately, this team, with a collective century-plus of climbing experience, maintained a closed system throughout the descent, preempting a more serious accident.

In Bohanon's analysis, the accident might have been prevented by: 1. Using a traditional double rope rappel on matching dynamic ropes; 2. Using a larger stopper knot like a figure eight or double fisherman for the knot block; 3. Rappelling the uneven-diameter dynamic and static ropes together using an ATC-style device; 4. Tying tighter into the retrieval line. (*Source: Tom Bohanon.*)

FALL ON SKIS | Failure to Adequately Assess Conditions
San Juan Mountains, Wilson Peak

On April 20, my partner Scott and I, Alec Orenstein (37), attempted a ski descent of the northeast face (the "Coors Couloir") of 14,017-foot Wilson Peak near Telluride. We began our approach via Silver Pick Basin at around 4 a.m. Changing over to crampons, we climbed a short couloir with steep snow and a fourth-class move that topped out on the southwest ridge of Wilson, and then traversed the ridge (with another fourth-class move) to reach the summit at around 11:30 a.m.

At the top, we encountered a skier and splitboarder who had passed us on the way up. They said they had traversed down the ridges along both sides of the northeast face but could not find a way to enter the face due to low snow coverage. They began to descend via the southwest ridge, the same way we had come up.

Scott and I descended the westerly of these ridges and stopped above what we believe is the usual entrance to the Coors Couloir. We discussed the coverage and concluded it would be safer to try to descend the northeast face with skis than to reverse the southwest ridge. Part of our thinking was that the other party included a snowboarder, who we judged would have had a much tougher time side-stepping down the top of the couloir, possibly explaining why they turned back.

I went first and began side-stepping down the face. I had my ski poles in my right (down-hill) hand, lashed together with a ski strap, and my ice axe in my left (uphill) hand, self-belaying with each step. I kicked off a small dry loose avalanche at the top, which did not reveal any more rocks below.

About 15 feet below the ridge, I had to move left above a rock band toward what looked like a safe zone where I could wait for Scott. I released my edges slightly to side-slip left and immediately hit several large rocks. I released from both bindings (even though I had locked the toes of my tech bindings), fell face-first into the rock band below me, and began sliding fast down the couloir.

About to drop in on the northeast face of Wilson Peak. The oval marks the start of a 1,200-foot fall. *Alec Orenstein*

I tumbled approximately 1,200 feet and came to rest in a large 35° snowfield below the couloir. I never lost consciousness. After taking a moment to assess my injuries, I called up to Scott to let him know I was conscious. Given my injuries and the fact that I had lost both skis in the valley hundreds of feet below me, I knew I wouldn't be able to descend back to the car, so I called my wife with my cell phone to tell her about the accident, and she called San Miguel County Search and Rescue.

It took Scott more than two hours to descend to me (he had to put his crampons back on to descend on foot). The SAR team had arranged a helicopter to do a rescue, and at SAR's direction and with Scott's heroic help, I part-glissaded, part-stumbled to a flat spot about 200 vertical feet below, where a helicopter was able to pick me up.

My injuries were more minor than they could have been. I broke the transverse processes of two of my lower vertebrae, two ribs, and the iliac crest of my pelvic bone. I suffered a small pneumothorax and deep cuts and abrasions on my torso, legs, and face. I spent the night in the hospital and was mostly recovered after about eight weeks.

ANALYSIS

In retrospect, we obviously shouldn't have tried to descend the couloir on skis, given the thin coverage. The party ahead of us clearly knew better. I have experience on alpine rock and scrambling, and I am an expert skier with experience in the backcountry, but this was my first ski-mountaineering expedition. Scott had more experience on this type of terrain than me, but ultimately our lack of experience judging the snowpack proved costly, especially on a route where the descent is on a different aspect than the approach.

The skiing was very much within our abilities, and we did make some good decisions that day, principally to wear helmets—in my case, a stout, heavy ski helmet.

The very lightweight climbing helmet that I had debated bringing probably would not have protected me from the repeated blows to the head I received. We carried full avalanche gear, and I believe the fully assembled shovel in my large backpack saved me from a more severe back injury. We also got an early start, leaving plenty of daylight for the eventual rescue. Although I ended up having perfect cell service from the mountain, I also had a Garmin inReach Mini that I could have used to call for help. (*Source: Alec Orenstein.*)

LOWERING ERROR | Rope Too Short, No Stopper Knot
Rifle Mountain Park, Project Wall

On May 22, a climber fell approximately 40 feet to the ground while being lowered from The Eighth Day (160 feet, 5.13a). This classic pitch is located on the Project Wall and has chains mid-route for a double-lower or rappels. While the climber was being lowered, the rope went through his belayer's device, and he fell, suffering unspecified serious injuries.

ANALYSIS
This accident likely would have been prevented with minimal research (the guidebook and other published descriptions make it very clear that two lowers or rappels are necessary to descend The Eighth Day) or a knot in the belayer's end of the rope. According to reporting in *Gym Climber*, the leader climbed the pitch with a 70m rope. While this is not specifically relevant to The Eighth Day (an 80m rope still won't get you down with one lower), it is worth noting that routes in certain sport climbing areas are getting longer and longer. In any case, there are very few circumstances in single-pitch climbing where you do not want a stopper knot in the end of the rope to close the system. (*Sources: Gymclimber.com.*)

TOP-ROPE SOLOING FALL | Device Unclipped from Rope
Montezuma, Haus Rock

On the morning of September 19, Craig Faulhaber (41) fell to the ground while top-rope-soloing Burning Down the Haus (5.13d). This 45-foot, slightly overhanging sport route is located on Haus Rock near Keystone, Colorado. Faulhaber, a climber with 12 years of experience, set up his system using a single strand of 9.5mm dynamic rope. He fixed the rope and descended using a Petzl Grigri, clipping the rope into one bolt near the top as a directional on the overhanging route.

For a self-belay, he switched to a Petzl Shunt attached to his harness' belay loop with a locking, anti-cross-loading carabiner. As he climbed, Faulhaber tied overhand stopper knots as backups. The rope was weighted at the base by water bottles and shoes to allow the Shunt to run smoothly up the rope. He worked the moves for most of the morning, falling about 30 times without incident. In a Mountain Project post, Faulhaber wrote, "I try the section, fall on the Shunt, brush, lower, try again, repeat." He linked the moves and decided to try the crux sequence again. This ten-foot section of V8 crimping required twisting and high-stepping about 30 feet off the ground. Faulhaber recalls, "I finally got the sequence and was pretty happy, looked down at a fellow climber who was watching to express some psych, and decided to try one more time."

This time Faulhaber fell, and in the process, his Shunt became disconnected from the rope. After 35 feet of free-fall, he landed on hard-packed dirt and rocks. Other climbers at the crag called 911, and Summit County Rescue Group responded. He was transported via ambulance to Keystone Medical Center and then helicoptered to St. Anthony's Hospital in Denver. Faulhaber sustained multiple broken bones, including L1 and L2 vertebrae, both heels, right elbow, pelvis, sacrum, and ribs.

Clip from a video demonsration showing how the Shunt can flip upside down and catch the rope in such a way that it releases under load. Heed the manufacturer's instructions: Do not use the Shunt as a solo top-rope device. *Yann Camus | BlissClimbing.com*

ANALYSIS

First and foremost, do not use the Petzl Shunt for solo top-roping. The Shunt is designed to use below a rappel device as a back-up, replacing a friction hitch like the prusik. [*There was a very similar incident in West Virginia this year. See page 91.*]

Faulhaber's Shunt and locking carabiner were still properly attached to his belay loop. The rope and stopper knots were intact. His last stopper knot was about six feet below where he fell. But the Shunt had somehow cleanly detached from the rope.

Faulhaber had researched different devices and solo techniques. He chose the Shunt after seeing it recommended on a blog/video by a professional climber. Though climbers have used the Shunt for solo top-roping since the 1980s, it was generally understood that it should only be used where the rope hangs straight down on vertical or less than vertical terrain. The Petzl website states that the Shunt is not recommended for self-belay for many reasons, including but not limited to the risk of the device's cam jamming in an overhanging or traversing situation.

Though Petzl has discouraged self-belay use since 2012, Faulhaber purchased a Shunt that featured a pre-2012 technical notice. The attached diagram showed a climber ascending a fixed line in vertical terrain with the Shunt. It also featured a diagram discouraging ascending a rope in overhanging terrain. Today, some retail websites that sell climbing gear still feature this older technical notice, and may even still recommend the Shunt for ascending.

The best Faulhaber can surmise is that the gymnastic twisting and high-stepping positions on the overhanging crux contributed to the accident. The device showed minimal deformation upon later inspection.

The most plausible theory is that the device turned sideways just below Faulhaber's waist as he high-stepped. There may have been enough friction in the system to create slack above the device, catching the rope in a sideways position as he fell. Instead of the Shunt's camming unit engaging, the rope may have caught in the small channel between the camming unit and the outer edge of the device's frame. This might have created large and unparallel forces that shock-loaded the device, allowing it to flex, and thus releasing the rope.

The best illustration of this phenomenon, referred to as the "Scorpion Catch" (because the twisted rope looks like a scorpion's tail), can be found on climbing guide Yann Camus' YouTube page or with the online version of this report. Again, Petzl clearly states that the Shunt is designed to be used only as a rappel backup and not for top-rope soloing. (*Sources: Craig Faulhaber, Mountain Project, Climbing Magazine, and the Editors.*)

AUTO-BELAY FATALITY
Northern Colorado

On June 12, a woman (57) died after falling 40 feet while climbing indoors. She appeared to have either become disconnected from an auto-belay or failed to clip into it. A police investigation found no fault in the equipment.

ANALYSIS
Though fatal accidents at indoor climbing gyms are extremely rare, there have been multiple cases involving auto-belays. In 2014, conservationist Mark Hesse died in a similar accident in Colorado. In 2021, a young climber died after falling 43 feet from an auto belay–equipped route in Sydney, Australia. Also in 2021, a 73-year-old man was seriously injured at a gym in Poland, falling 30 feet after his auto-belay line reportedly broke.

Don't become complacent. While auto-belays are great tools, they can present serious risk. Use them as if you were climbing with a partner by doing your own partner check. Before climbing, give a sharp upward tug after clipping in to the auto-belay to verify the connection, just as one might do after loading a Grigri to belay. (*Sources: Mountain Project, Gymclimber.com, 9News, Owen Clarke.*)

LEADER FALL | Belay Anchor Failure
Eldorado Canyon State Park, Wind Tower

On August 26, two climbers fell over 100 feet from Wind Ridge (4 pitches, 5.7). Climber 1 was in his 20s and survived with severe injuries. Climber 2 was in his 30s. He sustained fatal injuries.

The pair had climbed the first pitch of Tigger (5.6), followed by the second pitch of Wind Ridge. The second-pitch belay occupies a large ledge and offers a walk-off descent. The team opted for two more pitches (the last "pitch" being an easy traverse to a two-bolt rappel station). In a *Climbing* magazine accident report, Climber 1 recalled using a cordelette to girth-hitch a horn in the alcove for a belay.

Climber 1 began leading the third pitch, which starts with awkward and strenuous moves into a large hueco. He exited the hueco and moved up, at which point he gave his belayer a warning and fell.

An eyewitness, Aubrey Runyon, was climbing below. She heard Climber 1 shout "Falling!" before plummeting and yanking the belayer off the ledge. The two climbers tumbled end over end until they stopped on a ledge with a tree above the first pitch of a route called Tagger.

Runyon had extensive search and rescue experience in Colorado and Arizona. She built a gear anchor in the crack she was climbing and immediately called 911. She then lowered to the fallen climbers. (Runyon's belayer was still on the ground.)

Runyon saw that Climber 1 had a severely injured leg and wrist. He was in shock. Runyon was able to pick him up and put him on the ledge and stop the bleeding. She checked the other climber, who was tangled up in a tree. He was already deceased.

Rocky Mountain Rescue Group (RMRG) arrived at the base of the climb, ten minutes

The second-pitch belay anchor on Wind Ridge is best built with this large block, in this case using part of the lead rope to tie it off. The long sling in the foreground is clipped to a cam placed in a shallow pocket. *Pete Takeda*

after the 911 call. By then, Runyon had fixed ropes for the responders to facilitate a quicker rescue.

ANALYSIS

Eldorado Canyon is notorious for its heady climbing style and demanding terrain. Adventure often extends into the realm of gear placements and, in this case, belay anchors. The second-pitch belay of Wind Ridge offers few obvious anchor options to the uninitiated. Though there are multiple possibilities, the best is a large block requiring a very long cordelette or using a climbing rope as a tie-off. Both these practices, while standard on routes of similar grade/length, are often not used by neophytes or those transitioning into trad from other disciplines. The block also positions the belayer in an inconvenient spot [see photo above]. The very size of the ledge can lull climbers into a false sense of security. The last point might explain this tragedy.

Runyon found no gear clipped to the rope between Climber 1 and Climber 2, indicating there may have been no intermediate protection between the two climbers at the moment of the fall. Later, SAR found no evidence of an anchor at the belay ledge. Perhaps the pair were unanchored. Perhaps their gear came unclipped or broke, as can happen in severe incidents. What is certain is their anchor, assuming they had one, was insufficient.

This exact spot was the site of an eerily similar accident several months prior [see report below]. One takeaway from this tragedy is that classic Eldorado climbs may ask more from the novice climber than the "easy" grade and endless queues at the base might indicate. (Sources: Gymclimber.com, Aubrey Runyon.)

LEADER FALL | Single Piece Pulled Out
Eldorado Canyon State Park, Wind Tower

My partner Mike (46) and I, Tiffany Hauck (50), convened on the morning of June 13. Our sights were set on Wind Ridge (4 pitches, 5.7). We had climbed on the route a month earlier but ended up missing a good portion of the ridge. We wanted to bag the full climb.

We made good progress and were soon at the top of the second pitch, nested in a cave-like hollow. Mike had led the previous pitch and opted to wrap the rope around a single largish boulder as the only anchor in the belay. I'd led the next pitch previously and knew that once I maneuvered past the chin-up, it was gravy.

I tightened my helmet and stepped onto a nearby boulder, so I could stretch and reach a large flake, which overhangs about eight feet above the belay. I heaved myself up into a narrow hollow. I put a cam in the same crack I'd previously used and then yanked in four directions. Satisfied the cam was stable and wouldn't walk, I clipped in, stood up, assessed my position, and made a step onto a tiny foothold—and I slipped. My right side slammed onto a large boulder at the edge of the belay ledge and I bounced—how far out, I don't know, as I lost sense of direction. [As *Hauck fell, the sole cam she had placed as protection pulled out.*] My ears filled with the sound of pro slamming into the rock and striking my helmet. I was yanked back toward the rock, then bounced briefly again before I came to a stop. [*Hauck and her partner estimated the fall was around 30 feet, ending well below the belay ledge.*]

It took time, but I righted myself and looked up to see Mike leaning over the boulder I'd hit on the way down. The first thing I noticed was a large splatter of blood on the rock between us, but Mike quickly explained that it was his blood—he had been pulled violently across

Wind Ridge climbs directly to the circled belay ledge atop pitch two. From here, climbers can either escape left or continue through an overhang, the site of both falls reported here. In August, two climbers fell all the way to the point marked X (see previous page). *Tommy Copeland*

the rock when I fell. I painfully climbed back to the belay ledge, and eventually we scrambled over to the descent trail. With the help of Mike and a climber named Hillary, who had come up the route behind us, I was able to walk out under my own power.

A visit to the emergency room revealed no concussion and no broken bones. I had minor scrapes and bruises on my shins, and contusions on my hip and buttocks. That evening, my left shin swelled to twice its normal size. The contusion would take weeks to heal.

ANALYSIS

It is hard to say for sure the cause of the cam failing. I don't know if it's because I put in the wrong sized cam or if I put it in a bad location. But the most likely cause is that I placed too small of a cam, or that I placed it in a flaring crack. (*Source: Tiffany Hauck.*)

Editor's Note: *The cracks available at the crux are flared and piton-scarred, making cam placements tricky. A fall here is often a ledge fall. One can easily walk off from here by traversing the big ledge.*

FALL ON ROCK | Tumble After Rappel
Eldorado Canyon State Park, West Ridge

I, Beth Sager (40), uneventfully led Chianti (5.8+), a route I had previously climbed. My partner Sylwia followed, and then I rappelled while she waited at the anchor. My friends Jane and Ilyse were on a route next door. I took myself off rappel 20 feet above the ground on a ledge that marks the beginning of the actual climbing after a third-class scramble.

I noticed that the end of the rope was caught in a constriction several feet below. As I leaned forward to free it, I lost my balance and tumbled to the ground, hitting the rock several times. I was still wearing my helmet. My friends came down as quickly as they could and checked me for a concussion or other injuries. Though I was shaken up and had pain in my neck, I was able to walk out and drive myself to the ER. My friend, who had driven separately, followed in her car to make sure I was okay. I was found to have a fracture of my C1 vertebra in addition to multiple scrapes, bruises, and a sprained finger. I did not have a concussion. My neck healed within six weeks, but my sprained finger is still problematic ten months later.

ANALYSIS

There was no reason to free the rope in the way I attempted. Sylwia could have rappelled without any problem, and we could have freed the stuck rope while descending. I was simply not being mindful of the terrain. I'm extremely lucky that I wasn't hurt worse, because the ground where I fell was uneven. (*Source: Beth Sager.*)

FALL ON ROCK | Climbing Unroped
Eldorado Canyon State Park, Rincon

On October 6 at approximately 5:45 p.m., four climbers called 911 to report a fallen male climber, later identified as Scott Dewey, 31 years old, near Rincon Wall in

Eldorado Canyon. The climber was alone without a rope, harness, or gear and was presumed to be free soloing. There was no evidence of rockfall at the scene. There were no witnesses to the fall, and the exact route that Dewey was climbing isn't known. Dewey was found unconscious, not breathing, and had no pulse. He was declared deceased later that day.

ANALYSIS

While the details of Dewey's accident are not known, unroped climbing is inherently hazardous. According to the victim's personal Mountain Project page, he began free soloing regularly several months before his accident. Most of the routes he had climbed unroped were ones which he had previously redpointed. Even so, the routes were only a few grades below those which he was typically leading. This style holds much greater consequences than other forms of climbing, and it is a personal choice of whether or not to accept those risks. (*Sources: GymClimber.com, The Editors.*)

STRANDED | Unsure of Descent Route
Eldorado Canyon State Park, Redgarden Wall

About 8:20 p.m. on December 4, the Boulder County Sheriff's Office received a phone call from two climbers who were stuck near the top of Redgarden Wall, the highest cliff in Eldorado Canyon. The climbers, who were from Manitou Springs and Fort Collins, had started climbing at 10 a.m. and neared the top at dusk. They were unsure of the route back down from Redgarden, which, depending on the climb, is either by complex scrambling or a series of rappels.

Rocky Mountain Rescue Group arrived on the scene and were able to reach the climbers at 9:40 p.m., after climbing up the East Slabs descent route. Both climbers were assisted down the East Slabs.

Exactly two weeks later, on December 18, the Boulder County Communications Center received a 911 call from two climbers near the top of Redgarden. The pair were stranded, close to hypothermic, and in need of rescue. The climbers, a 28-year-old male and a 30-year-old male, both from Denver, began climbing around 11:30 a.m. As with the prior incident, they did not reach the top until around dusk and were uncertain of the descent route.

Rescuers from the Rocky Mountain Rescue Group climbed the East Slabs and reached the climbers at approximately 9:40 p.m. The two climbers were assisted off the southwest face of Tower One and then down to the road. The climbers were uninjured. The rescue took approximately six hours.

ANALYSIS

Many climbers have been stranded on top of this large, complex formation. For this reason, it's very helpful to climb your first Redgarden route with a partner who knows the descent routes. If that's not possible, thorough research of the descent options is essential, as is an early start and conservative climbing schedule, especially during the short days of winter. See "Know The Ropes" in this edition for more discussion of complex descents. (*Sources: Boulder County Sheriff's Office, Boulder Daily Camera.*)

BELAYER PULLED INTO CLIMBING WALL
Denver

On July 23, I broke my foot and ankle in two places while belaying another climber. I was working with a nonprofit at a Denver multisport event involving disabled veterans. I set up their mobile climbing wall to use with a gentleman who had had a stroke the year before. He had hemiplegia (a form of paralysis that's a common after-effect of a stroke) resulting in severe weakness on the right side. For climbers such as himself, I set up a top-rope with a static rope so I can provide a power belay, without dynamic stretch.

The man was able to lift and grip a bit with his right hand. He was much bigger than me, and when asked he claimed to weigh 245 pounds. I weigh 145, so I was not concerned about the difference. He climbed to about two feet from the top (22 feet total) when he slipped and fell back hard. I was standing three feet from the center line to keep the rope off his back. When he fully weighted the rope, I slid over the gravel and was lifted like I'd held a leader fall. I quickly put my foot up to stop myself on the wall. The force fractured my heel and navicular bone. My doctor believes I was slightly off center and my foot hit at a weird angle. Had I hit flat, it would have been fine.

I didn't want the man to know he had injured me, so I lowered him and sat down. He wanted to climb again, so I put him on an auto-belay. Once he was finished, I told a staff member my foot was broken. I hopped away, got a ride to my car, and drove to the ER in Fort Collins.

ANALYSIS
Later I looked at the man's online registration form, and he had listed his weight as 320 pounds. If I had known that he weighed more than twice as much as me, I would have anchored myself to the base before belaying and maybe used an Edelrid Ohm to reduce the impact force of any fall. I also might have kept my shoulder against the wall so that the force was up, not up and in.

But the main takeaway is, if the climber is much bigger than you, anchor yourself before belaying, even for a top-rope. Protect yourself at all costs. (*Source: Craig DeMartino, age 56.*)

Editor's Note: DeMartino's lower right leg was amputated after a climbing accident almost 20 years ago. He is the first amputee to climb El Capitan in under a day and is a two-time National Adaptive Climbing Champion.

FATAL ROCKFALL | Possible Wildlife Origin
Clear Creek Canyon, Other Critters Crag

On December 4, a male climber (28) was struck by a falling rock while waiting at the base of the first pitch of Tortoise Scute (5.6), a three-pitch bolted climb. The block was reportedly microwave-sized. Although he survived the initial impact (he was wearing a helmet), he was later taken off life support at the hospital.

ANALYSIS
The rockfall initially was believed to have been generated by climbers above. However, it is improbable that a falling object dropped by climbers would have intersected the

The Other Critters cliff in Clear Creek Canyon attracts both two- and four-legged climbers. Bighorn sheep may have dislodged the rock that caused a fatality in December. The arrow marks the start of Tortoise Scute, where the climber was struck. *Alan Prehmus*

base of Tortoise Scute, as most of this crag's climbs and the walk-off descent route are far to the west of Tortoise Scute, and no climbers are believed to have been directly above the route at the time of the accident.

Evidence points to a natural event, quite possibly wildlife-generated rockfall. Climber Scott Turpin, who established highlines and climbs at a crag west of Other Critters and built a trail used to access these areas, said he frequently saw bighorn sheep in the area. "Especially in the winter and spring, bighorns would use the trail frequently, but were more often on the opposite side, directly above Safari and Other Critters. I saw lambs with them on multiple occasions. Though I was impressed by how agile the sheep were, I definitely saw them trundle rocks."

Colorado Parks and Wildlife senior wildlife biologist Shannon Schaller said, "Bighorns frequent Clear Creek Canyon. It's a lambing area, and they very possibly could have dislodged a rock above the climbing cliff." She notes, "Rocks triggered by bighorns are a potential hazard to climbers, though it's extremely rare as the sheep are very shy and tend to avoid people." Nonetheless, she said, "I personally have seen falling rock caused by wildlife. For the same reasons people like to climb in an area, it's also good for a bighorn habitat."

It's easy to be lulled into a sense of security at a very popular crag. The moderate grades, easy access, and sun-drenched aspect make this particular cliff a busy year-round destination. However, this is not a gym, and natural rockfall should be expected at any crag in a mountainous or canyon environment. (This is especially true after heavy rain or snow or during wind storms, all of which can dislodge rocks.) Adopting an alpinist's sense of mountain awareness can help prevent such accidents. Watch and listen for rockfall, try to choose protected belay areas, and wear helmets while climbing, belaying, or waiting your turn to climb. (*Sources: Mountain Project, Scott Turpin, and Shannon Schaller.*)

FALL ON ROCK | Off Route, Exceeding Abilities
Clear Creek Canyon, Anarchy Wall

In mid-November, "Bill," a climber in his mid-30s, took a serious leader fall after going off route while attempting a sport route called Power Trip (5.12a).

According to a witness, Bill had mentioned climbing 5.12 in the gym but was shaky upon starting the route. He was part of a large group accompanied by dogs, and the witness was concerned about the group's ability to climb without distraction. Bill drifted off route, missed a clip, and became very run-out. When he fell, his right foot was behind the rope, causing him to flip upside down and pendulum. His head impacted first. He lowered and after a short period began exhibiting signs of mild concussion and complaining about neck pain. He departed the crag. It is unknown whether he received medical attention.

ANALYSIS
Crowding at a crag degrades clear communication and creates an environment in which peer pressure and overconfidence can foment hazardous conditions. These circumstances may have resulted in Bill continuing to attempt the climb even though he was off route. His belayer caught the fall as well as could be expected given the circumstances—Bill fell down half of the route while upside down. Thankfully, even though the route was short and often climbed as a warmup for this difficult crag, Bill was wearing a helmet. His helmet was visibly damaged but did not crack. Had he not been wearing the helmet, his injuries may have been far more severe. (*Source: Anonymous.*)

ROCKFALL, AVALANCHE
Front Range, Torreys Peak

On June 6, a group (undisclosed number) of climbers preparing for a trip to the Pacific Northwest camped near the Stevens Gulch trailhead for Grays and Torreys peaks. They planned to start early the next morning in order to practice rope and snow-travel skills on steep, snow-covered terrain. They left the trailhead about 4:30 a.m. and followed the summer trail into the alpine area below the east face of 14,267-foot Torreys Peak. They formed a single roped group and began ascending Dead Dog Couloir, a classic gully that's often skied in the spring. They moved up the initial snow slope as a rope team, placing snow pickets.

At 8:15 a.m. they were about halfway up the couloir and stopped for a short break. They had started moving up the couloir again when, shortly before 8:55 a.m., a section of rock on the climber's right side of the couloir detached, showering the group with rocks and releasing a small loose-wet avalanche. The elevation was 13,500 feet, with a slope angle of 40°.

One of the climbers was hit by moving debris but traveled only a short distance down the slope. Two of the climbers were struck by rocks; one was injured. The group provided first-aid to the injured climber. Two Flight for Life helicopters dropped SAR teams, but the entire group traveled back to the trailhead without assistance.

This incident occurred on an east-facing route in early June, and as such it warmed up rapidly when the sun hit. The group got a fairly early start, but they knew they'd be moving slowly since they were going to be roped. The accident happened almost 4.5 hours after they started hiking, and they were still fairly low in the couloir. This suggests they should have started considerably earlier for safer travel. The Colorado Avalanche Information Center said that warmer temperatures were loosening the rock and snow, making for treacherous conditions. "Anywhere there's snow, there's potential for an avalanche," said Ethan Greene, director at CAIC, to CBS4. "If you're heading into alpine areas, there's loose rock and loose snow. It's beautiful weather, but you have to be careful." (*Source: Colorado Avalanche Information Center, CBS4.*)

The Dead Dog Couloir on Torreys Peak, showing (A) origin of the rockfall and (B) location of the party hit by a rock and snow avalanche. *Colorado Avalanche Information Center*

ROCK COLLAPSE BEFORE FIRST BOLT
Shelf Road, Cactus Cliff

On August 8, an unidentified climber fell approximately 40 feet to the ground when the rock beneath his feet collapsed. The climber was scrambling up the 4th-class ramp leading to the first bolt of The Joy of Cholla (5.11d), a one-pitch sport route on the popular Cactus Cliff.

According to a comment posted at Mountain Project the day after the accident, "over 1,000 pounds of rock" reportedly came off, and the climber was airlifted to the hospital, after suffering serious injuries. He was expected to fully recover.

ANALYSIS

This was one of several serious accidents last year involving rockfall on established and well-traveled crags. While Shelf Road's limestone is generally sound, the area has its share of loose, fractured, and decomposed rock. Stay alert and test the rock when uncertain, especially when protection (as in this case) is absent. [*Editor's Note: Two bolts were added to protect this approach ramp in January 2022.*] (*Source: Mountain Project.*)

IDAHO

LOWERING ERROR | Failure to Retie Correctly
City of Rocks, Decadent Wall

On June 20, Peter (65), Vivien (52), and Amy (50) intended to climb Another Greg Lowe Route (5.8, trad) and then top-rope a neighboring 5.10a climb. All three were veteran climbers, with collective experience exceeding 100 years, and all had been accident-free until the day of this incident.

Peter led the 5.8 pitch and was lowered from an anchor 50 feet to the ground. Vivien clipped into the middle of the rope with a "double figure 8" knot on her locking belay carabiner, and ascended the route to the belay chains. Another party arrived at the base of the climb, intending to climb the same route. Peter then asked Vivien to rig the single anchor to allow both parties to use the anchor. Vivien yelled, "Take." Peter attempted to take up slack and observed Vivien freefalling to the ground.

Vivien struck the ground only seven feet away from Peter. The surface was relatively flat sand and grass. Vivien was conscious and breathing, but confused. Peter was a physician and was able to determine she had a pelvis and hip fracture and may have sustained internal injuries. Peter immobilized her neck and pelvis, as best he could, and yelled for help. There was no cell phone service at this location. Two climbers on the ground were sent to notify the National Park Service headquarters of the accident.

Two other climbers (rangers Austin Palmieri and Nate Ament from Arches National Park) were climbing an adjacent route. They had a Garmin inReach and were able to send a distress signal. The rangers relayed that a medical helicopter evacuation was urgently required, and that a suitable landing zone was available only 200 yards away. The helicopter arrived within 20 minutes, and Vivien was transported to Portneuf Medical Center in Pocatello, Idaho.

Vivien suffered a cardiac arrest just after arrival at the hospital and miraculously survived a complex resuscitation, which involved transfusions greater than three times her blood volume, and two trips to the operating room. At the time this report was written, four months after the accident, Vivien was neurologically intact, walking, swimming, and continued to be committed to her rehabilitation. She had no recall of the accident.

ANALYSIS

This accident occurred through failure of the climber to retie her knot after reconfiguring her anchor. Vivien was not attached to the climbing rope when she fell. Human error played a role, with contributing factors including: 1) Vivien had tied into the middle of the rope, not her usual procedure; 2) Another party arrived, wishing to ascend the same climb, creating some feeling of time pressure; 3) Peter asked Vivien to rig the anchor such that two parties could use it, and believes his request was distracting; 4) Vivien untied from the middle of the rope while rigging the anchor and failed to tie back in; 5) Vivien called "take," but it's believed she did not wait for the pull of the rope or weight-test the system. Given the extent of her injuries, Vivien was fortunate that another party nearby was able to contact EMS with their satellite communication device, which likely saved her life. (*Source: Peter Lenz.*)

KENTUCKY

GROUND FALL | Off Route, No Protection
Red River Gorge, Long Wall

On March 12, after onsighting Mailbox (5.8, trad) and Rock Wars (5.10a, trad)—both fantastic routes—my friends and I wanted to continue climbing on something easier. We found a climb called Long Wall Chimney (5.7, trad). I (male, 22) racked up and checked Mountain Project for info on the route.

I noticed a giant loose chockstone at the start that seemed like it might be necessary to pull on to get established in the crack. I opted for a start on the face to the left to avoid the chockstone. The move was extremely committing (almost like pulling a roof with a mantel onto the face). I made one or two moves and found myself stuck. I could not traverse right into the crack, as it would involve using the awful chockstone, and I couldn't move up because the rock was featureless. At this point, I was about 10 feet off the ground with no gear placed. I began to downclimb and almost slipped. I decided the only option was to jump, so my friends cleared the landing and spotted me for the fall.

I committed to the jump and landed perfectly flat-footed on my left foot. Due to having so much gear on my harness and landing with all the weight on one foot, I immediately felt an awful shooting pain in my entire foot. I fell over and lay on my back to see if the pain would dissipate. I removed my climbing shoes and other gear and waited. About 30 minutes passed, and the foot was now swelling quickly. I couldn't put any weight on it, so the only option was to carry me out. My friend, and coworker at the time, Diego, picked me up and carried me like a backpack about 80 percent of the Long Wall access trail. I was able to crab walk on the steeper sections.

I found out about a week later that I had a Lisfranc fracture (the space between the big and second toe) in my left foot. I couldn't walk for three months, and I still have lingering pain despite months of PT. All of this was because I did the wrong start to a 5.7, and with it being a trad route, I had no way to "take."

ANALYSIS

I learned from the accident to always check and double-check the correct start of a route if unsure (especially true for unprotected trad). Later, I discovered from a comment on Mountain Project that another climber had fallen six feet to the ground while attempting the same start to avoid the chockstone. They also commented that the rest of the party used the chockstone without an issue. (Source: Adam Gallimore.)

Editor's Note: According to another climber at the crag that day, the chockstone was stable and used by other parties. The climber may have been able to reach a stance to assess the stone before making his decision. The takeaway is, it's better to avoid the route altogether than resort to an alternative start that's proven to cause—in this case at least—lasting injury.

LOWERING ERROR | Unclipped from Directional Rope

Red River Gorge, Bald Rock Recreational Preserve

In March, Logan Zhang (11) hit a boulder on the ground while cleaning a route in the Motherlode. Logan was using the cable car (a.k.a. tram) method to retrieve his draws, staying clipped to the belayer's side of the rope, as is common when cleaning overhanging routes. The first draw on the route was a permadraw so the climber didn't need to clean it. After he finished cleaning his draws from the route, Zhang continued lowering with the belayer's rope still running through the first draw. Before reaching the ground, he removed the tram draw from the belayer's rope and fell, hitting a boulder below the climb. He suffered a minor head laceration.

ANALYSIS

It is common for climbers to use the cable car or tram method to clean their draws off steep routes. It is important to understand the system and the consequences of adjustments. This incident could have been avoided by keeping the tram draw connected until the climber had reached the ground. Removing the tram draw when the climber is far from an overhanging wall instantly introduces slack into the system and the climber will drop. Also, remember to knot the end of the rope to close the system; the tram method uses more rope than standard lowering.

Alternatively, Logan could have removed the tram draw when he cleaned the quickdraw at the second bolt and taken the swing from this location, if it was safe to do so. This situation is not uncommon. Many climbers choose to leave their own draw on the first bolt for safety or efficiency when cleaning overhanging routes. See the 2021 "Know the Ropes" in *Accidents* (available at publications.americanalpineclub.org) for more information on cleaning steep climbs. (*Source: Ocean Zhang, father of Logan.*)

The tram method is an efficient way to clean quickdraws from overhanging climbs. Just be careful where you unclip the tram draw. *Lindsay Auble* [Inset] Logan's rendering of the accident scene.

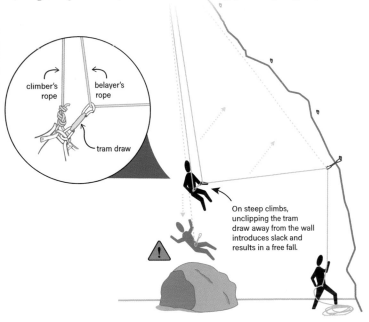

climber's rope | belayer's rope

tram draw

On steep climbs, unclipping the tram draw away from the wall introduces slack and results in a free fall.

FALL ON ROCK

Red River Gorge, Bald Rock Recreational Preserve

On December 4, a climber (male, 26) fell above the last piece of gear he had placed on Charlie (5.13b, single-pitch trad) at Chocolate Factory. The route follows a crack in a dihedral. The climber fell while making a dynamic move on the face of the over-hanging right wall. He took a long freefall that was arrested abruptly, hitting the left (vertical) face hard and resulting in a severe open fracture of the left tibia and fibula. The placed gear held.

The climber had been working this route for a couple of weeks. He took a similar fall while making the same move the day before with a different belayer. The fall that resulted in the injury was described as significantly longer than the previous fall and finished with an abrupt pendulum into the wall. The climber also felt like he came off the wall angled to the left. Both the climber and belayer have many years of experience.

ANALYSIS

Climber positioning during the fall likely contributed to the injury. It also appears the belayer may have had more slack in the system than appropriate and did not "move into" the fall enough when the rope tightened (to soften the arrest). With very steep climbs, common in the Southeast, some belayers can get in the habit of leaving out excessive slack, since a falling climber is unlikely to impact the wall with enough force to cause injury. While most of the climbing on Charlie is along the steeper right side of the dihedral, the belayer needs to consider that the climber may swing into the vertical left face during a fall and should soften the arrest appropriately.

It is a common misconception that extra slack equates to a soft catch. The slack lengthens a fall, but it is the belayer's movement into the fall as the rope tightens that softens the arrest. Learn more about dynamic belaying in the Essentials article "Dynamic Belaying: The Art of the Soft Catch" in the 2021 *Accidents* or at publications. americanalpineclub.org. (*Sources: The climber and the Editors.*)

MINNESOTA

RAPPEL ANCHOR FAILURE

Minnesota, Taylors Falls

On March 25, Climber 1 (31) and Climber 2 (23) were involved in a rock climbing accident at Interstate State Park in Taylors Falls, Minnesota. The accident occurred while rappelling, with both falling from near the top of the cliff. Climber 2 was killed in the accident, and Climber 1 was seriously injured.

Climber 1 had over a decade of climbing experience, including trad, sport, and alpine climbing, from Minnesota to Alaska. He had worked as an outdoor trip leader for the University of Minnesota, graduating with a degree in recreation administration and a minor in outdoor recreation and education.

Climber 2 had climbed indoors extensively, with some experience bouldering and sport climbing outdoors. He had been planning a road trip for the upcoming climbing season with his girlfriend. According to Climber 1, Climber 2 wanted to expand his skills in preparation for that trip. March 25 was intended to be the first in a series of mentoring outings.

On the way to the crag, the pair discussed goals for the day. Climber 2 wanted to focus on anchors and get introduced to trad gear. Upon arrival, the team spent 30 minutes discussing types of protection (nuts, hexes, and cams), along with the SERENE acronym for anchor building. They then walked to an adjacent crag and further discussed anchors at the base. After about an hour, they walked to the top of the cliff and built an anchor together to top-rope a popular route called The Bulge.

After lunch, they agreed on mini-pitching (breaking a single established rope length into two short pitches) an easy route and then finish the day by building an anchor and rappelling. They chose the nearby Sonny and

This pillar is a solid block about five feet high and a foot wide. It's estimated to weigh at least a ton. Climber 1: "The block appears to extend into the ground both at the bottom and back. In reality, it is completely separated and can be moved back and forth over an inch with only moderate effort." The failed cam placements are marked. *Climber 1*

Juanita (5.5, trad). The route is about 45 feet tall, with a large ledge 35 feet up.

Climber 1 had climbed Sonny and Juanita many times and led two short pitches to the top without incident. There, he built an anchor comprised of three small cams placed in a vertical crack at the back of a ledge. He tied all the pieces together with a cordelette and tied in direct. He then belayed Climber 2 to the top, where the latter tied in directly to the anchor and the pair set up the rappel. Climber 2 had limited rappel experience and wanted to gain more.

After safety checks, Climber 2 unclipped from the anchor and rappelled over the lip. Still connected to the anchor, Climber 1 leaned over the edge to watch his partner rappel. When Climber 2 was 10 feet below the lip, Climber 1 heard a loud cracking noise. He turned his head quickly enough to see the anchor gear snapping out of the crack. He was then pulled off of the ledge by his falling partner's weight.

He recalls, "I vaguely remember hitting the large ledge ten feet beneath me with the left side of my body before falling the rest of the way to the ground. I was knocked unconscious by the impact, landing just a few feet from where I tied in to do my very first climb nearly ten years before."

Many bystanders in this popular area responded, as Climber 1 fell in and out of consciousness. An ambulance arrived and he was driven to the hospital and then flown to a regional medical center. X-rays and CT scans revealed no major broken bones or internal injuries. He suffered two sprained ankles, a broken left foot, a severely dislocated left ring finger, abrasions, and a concussion. Climber 2 unfortunately died from the injuries suffered in the fall.

ANALYSIS

The rappel anchor was built with three cams in a single crack in the blocky basalt atop the cliff. The combined weight of Climber 2 rappelling and Climber 1 leaning off his tether to look over the edge was apparently enough to lever open the crack and cause the cams to fail.

Climber 1 recalled, "I have built over 1,000 anchors in rock, ice, and snow in my climbing career. I have never had a piece of protection, let alone a whole anchor, fail. I do remember testing the rock and it not moving, but regardless of how well I tested it, there was simply no reason to build the anchor in a single crack. There were other rock features in the area I could have used, along with at least one significant tree I could have included in the anchor."

He concluded, "Building an anchor with three pieces of protection does not necessarily mean that anchor is redundant. A redundant anchor should also use redundant features. This ensures that if one of the rock features fails, the other pieces remain intact."

Using multiple features to build an anchor is particularly important in an area like Taylors Falls, which is susceptible to severe freeze/thaw cycles and is known to have fractured rock. The top of the cliff is composed of exposed and often shattered basalt. Small rocks are routinely released from the cliff tops and faces, and at times entire rock formations have failed. (*Sources: Climber 1 and the Editors.*)

MONTANA

FALL ON ROCK | Inadequate Protection
Blodgett Canyon, Shoshone Spire

On June 21, Carson Broaddus (24) was climbing with Alexandra Stapleton (24) on the classic Shoshone South Face (5 pitches, 5.8+). The pair had linked pitches one and two. Broaddus was midway up pitch three, leading moderate 5th class on ledgy terrain between steeper sections. He climbed past a flat ledge, making some 5th-class moves, his last gear a number 3 Camalot about 12 feet below. He was traversing a few feet to place some gear when he pulled off a dinner-plate-size flake of granite with his right hand.

Broaddus tumbled 20 feet and struck the ledge with his right hip and lower back. He rolled off and fell another ten feet before swinging into the wall back first. His head hit and cracked his helmet in two. He suffered a Grade 2 hematoma on the right hip and deep bruising, a scalp laceration, and a severely sprained ankle.

With no cell service and no emergency communication device, Broaddus and his partner self-rescued. They built an emergency anchor, did two rappels to the base, and limped back to the trail. They hiked a mile and a half, at one point passing a hiker who ran for cell service and called emergency services. Four hours after the climbers started down, SAR arrived.

ANALYSIS

Runouts on poor rock flirt with disaster. The Shoshone South Face is a classic route on a beautiful multi-pitch spire, and the rock is generally solid. But as Mountain Project states, "The important thing to remember is you're climbing in Montana, and you're going to run into the choss sooner than later."

The South Face route on Shoshone Spire in Blodgett Canyon follows a direct line near the left skyline. *Steph Abegg*

In retrospect, Broaddus suggested placing more protection on ledgy terrain and testing all holds before trusting them with full weight. Given the damage to his helmet incurred in the fall, he also wrote, "Everyone has heard this before, but listen: Wear a helmet. I would be dead otherwise." (*Sources: Carson Broaddus, Mountain Project.*)

LONG FALL ON ROCK | Ledge Collapsed
Gallatin Canyon, The Watchtower

On July 16, Greg Sievers (63) and Rob Meshew (49) climbed a three-pitch route on the lower tier of the Watchtower in order to access Silver Foxes (3 pitches, 5.10a) on the upper tier. Sievers then started up the first pitch of Silver Foxes. The pitch had 11 bolts in 120 feet of climbing, with difficulties up to 5.7. It was well within his ability. At the 10th bolt, he moved right for a no hands stem rest on a 16-inch by four-inch ledge. There, 15 feet below the belay, the ledge suddenly collapsed.

"I was only able to get half the word 'falling' out of my mouth when the first impact caused my body to rotate and go horizontal," Sievers said. "Accelerating, I began to pendulum to the left. I had a fleeting thought of 'why wasn't I stopping' when my body took a massive impact 40 feet down on a small outside corner. I heard a loud CRACK from inside my back. The snapping was as audible as breaking a dry branch, which I assumed was a rib or two. Everything went black for a few brief seconds, but I did not lose consciousness."

Meshew was directly below. He was unscathed, despite the hundreds of pounds of rock that rained down around him. Busy dodging rocks, he unfortunately sent Sievers on a long fall. The latter wrote, "In a perfect world the fall would have been about 15 feet. But Rob was scrambling for his life. The sheer quantity of shrapnel coming at him was tremendous: lots of six-inch by one-inch pieces, plus a 200-pound block landed where he'd been standing." Sievers added, "I don't know how he avoided injury, but had he been hit, I may have taken a 90-footer all the way to the deck."

Meshew lowered Sievers to the ledge and they did an assessment of his injuries. Sievers then taped his foot to stabilize it. He belayed Meshew up the pitch to clean the gear and then decided to self-rescue rather than wait for a rescue. Sievers later said, "In hindsight I'm not convinced I made the right choice. An airlift would have likely been faster."

Sievers made three rappels down the lower tier using a kleimheist backup on the ropes. He was in pain but unaware that his back was broken. Once on the ground, the pair worked their way down the trail. That morning, they had done the 1.5 mile approach hike via the Lava Lake trailhead. Now, with the highway just on the other side of the river, and given his condition, Sievers believed his best option was to catch a ride across the Gallatin River from one of the many active commercial raft outfits. Sievers suggested Meshew descend ahead of him, take his motorcycle home, and return with his truck to collect Sievers. Meshew agreed and departed. Using a dry branch as a crutch, Sievers descended a rugged 400 feet to the climbers' trail and the Gallatin River. Eventually, a rafter ferried him to the other side of the river. Meshew arrived with the truck. Seven hours after the accident, Sievers was in a Bozeman ER.

Sievers was diagnosed with a broken T-11 vertebra, broken bones in his right ankle, a broken tibia base, and a possible head injury (TBI). In June 2022, Sievers wrote, "I'm looking at a second spinal surgery, and the neurosurgeon said I should give up climbing and skiing since my lumbar group has no discs left and is now bone on bone."

ANALYSIS
Serious falls often occur on "easy" terrain. It can happen to anyone at any time. With decades of climbing in all genres, Sievers was extremely experienced. He notes with some irony that, "After almost 40 years of climbing, some of it on very sketchy mixed alpine routes, this was my first serious fall—on a [expletive deleted] bolted 5.7 pitch."

In accidents like this, rock quality frequently comes into play. On Mountain Project, the first pitch of Silver Foxes is called "one of the best moderates in the canyon with amazing face climbing." Yet as this accident shows, rock quality can never be taken for granted, especially if you leave the most traveled line on a route, as Sievers did.

Finally, Meshew was belaying with a Black Diamond ATC-Guide. While such a device is versatile and adequate, had he been using an assisted-braking device, such as a Grigri, he might have been able to arrest Sievers' fall sooner while dodging the falling rocks. This might have "...saved me maybe 50 percent of the fall distance," wrote Sievers. "I remember him showing me his hand—the rope zipping through burned a line in his palm." (*Sources: Greg Sievers, Mountain Project.*)

FALL ON ICE | Exceeding Abilities, Ego Pressure
Hyalite Canyon, Unnamed Wall

On January 17, climbers W (18) and T (19) met at 7:30 a.m. to carpool into Hyalite Canyon. They had not previously climbed together. They planned to climb The Thrill is Gone, a classic M4 chimney on the popular and paradoxically named Unnamed Wall. W had been rock climbing for almost five years and ice climbing for three. T was very experienced on rock and had three years of ice climbing.

At the crag, T led Thrill and cleaned the route. W then re-led Thrill. As he climbed,

he noticed a bolted mixed route to the left and decided to attempt that route next. The guidebook identified it as Sharp Dressed Man (M6 R). Though often ice-covered, the route had ice only a third of the way down. W concluded the R rating was due to the bolts being iced over in most seasons. He was unfazed by the M6 rating, despite never having led that difficulty. T perhaps wisely declined to lead, but was happy to belay.

W climbed confidently up the initial section on positive and obvious holds. Fifteen feet up, below the first bolt, the holds became worse. W was not pumped and did not consider downclimbing. Instead, he placed his left tool on a precarious sloping

[Above] W climbing The Thrill Is Gone prior to embarking on Sharp Dressed Man. The latter climbs the rock to his left. A bolt is barely visible at the left edge of the image. [Inset] Makeshift splint made from ice tools, duct tape, and a borrowed ski strap.

edge and locked off. The clip was reachy, but he could not find other obvious holds. As W fumbled for a quickdraw his tool popped. He fell off the wall with a scream. W plummeted eight feet before striking a rocky ledge with his left foot. His crampon snagged on the rock and the foot caved inward. He fell the remaining distance, landing on his right foot in a soft patch of snow before rolling onto his tailbone and back.

His partner and some friends rushed over. W took off his left crampon without removing the boot. The rescuers made a makeshift splint with ice tools, duct tape, and a borrowed ski strap. With assistance from the other climbers and some butt scooting, W made it back to T's truck. The ER doctor, himself an ice climber, determined that W had broken bones in his ankle but most likely wouldn't need surgery.

ANALYSIS

When one is young and ambitious, it's not uncommon to push oneself hard, but pushing the limits on ice and mixed terrain can get out of control much faster than in other disciplines. In retrospect, W says, "The most striking error in the decision-making was my insistence on leading a difficult route with insufficient experience. Until this season I had almost exclusively climbed water ice. Though I managed a couple D6/7 top-ropes and a handful of thin ice leads earlier this year, I had never led a proper dry-tool route. Sharp Dressed Man was clearly outside my skill level, but I recall thinking I could easily climb it.

"I subconsciously believed that, because I hadn't fallen before, I wouldn't fall this time. In spite of several recent accidents in the community, I seemed to think I was somehow different and invulnerable. Equally influential was my ego and desire to be respected by the people around me—foremost my partner T. His wealth of experience, combined with the fact that we'd never climbed together before, made me eager to leave a good impression." [*Editor's Note: Sharp Dressed Man was first climbed by Alex Lowe and Jack Tackle in 1984. Those who are aware of their climbing record treat their routes with great deference.*]

W continued: "I incorrectly extrapolated that because the first few feet of bouldering felt easy, the remaining 60-plus feet would be the same. Furthermore, my consultation of the guidebook consisted of a quick scan and a glance at the photos. Had I actually taken the time to read the passage, I would have discovered [this route] was a popular top-rope and rarely iced over, earning its R rating from a runout above a final manky piton.

"The final flaw in my decision-making was my refusal to establish a safety net. As a good friend of mine said, I was 'free soloing until the first bolt.' Although I considered setting up a top-rope from the chains of Thrill, one of the first things to pass through my head was a concern for how I would be perceived. I also hadn't realized that stick-clipping was the preferred method to clip the first bolt.

"Reflecting on the accident, I see how much worse it could have been. I am so grateful for the medical training of my rescuers and their calm and efficient response." (*Source: W.*)

NEVADA

BOULDERING FALL | Poor Pad Placement
Red Rock, Kraft Boulders

On March 20, Alonso Rodriguez (25) was climbing Monkey Bar (V2) on the very popular Monkey Bar Boulder. He was part of a group of five, and a total of 15 climbers were at the boulder, with over ten crash pads. On his onsight attempt, Rodriguez fell off the last move. He plummeted ten feet, missed the pads with his right foot, and felt a sharp pain in his heel. He quickly sat down and pulled off his shoe—the foot was already starting to swell. His friends helped him out of the area, each taking turns carrying him on their backs.

At the hospital, Rodriguez was diagnosed with an ankle sprain, with a two- or three-week recovery. Three weeks later, still unable to walk, Rodriguez got a second opinion. New X-rays revealed a badly broken calcaneus. He has since recovered and returned to professional highlining, though he still suffers from arthritic pains. He stopped bouldering after the incident.

ANALYSIS

Many bouldering accidents result from inattentive or absent spotting and poor pad placement. Rodriguez recalled, "Clearly, my spotters were not attentive in any way, shape, or form. I thought when I let go, I'd be hitting soft pads. Instead, one foot landed on pads while the other smashed hard rock. I was also so hyped by the amount of people trying that I didn't think twice about it. In a sense, ego took over. I will never let that happen again. Safety is paramount in any outdoor activity, and ego is a danger to us all." (*Source: Alonso Rodriguez.*)

Close Call in Red Rock: On October 20, two climbers nearing the top of Epinephrine, the long 5.9 classic in Black Velvet Canyon, fell while simul-climbing. Three pieces of protection between the two pulled out during the fall, and the two tumbled toward the ground far below, stopping only when their rope snagged on a knob of sandstone. Simul-climbing is a useful technique for moving quickly on easy terrain, but it's essential that all placements of intermediate protection are bombproof. A short account of the dramatic rescue of these climbers is on page 121.

NEW HAMPSHIRE

SLIDING FALL ON SNOW | Inadequate Crampons
White Mountains, Mt. Washington

On March 14, at approximately 5:15 p.m., a winter climber took a long sliding fall while descending a steep section of the Lion Head Winter Route on Mt. Washington. He was part of a group of three who all carried ice axes but were wearing lightweight hiking boots with Microspikes-style traction devices. A local guide who was also a paramedic/ER nurse was descending with clients and witnessed the movements of the team of three, noting they were attempting to glissade in some places and scooting down on their butts in others. Shortly before the long fall, one of them slid some distance, in the process losing their ice axe, which the guide returned to them.

Above the rock step—a stretch of steep, often icy ledges about 30 feet high—another member of this party slipped, slid the length of the steep section, struck his head on a tree, was knocked unconscious, and sustained a six-inch laceration to the forehead, coming to rest in a patch of trees in the fall line below. The guide assisted his clients to safety, treated the patient, and then short-roped the injured climber down to walking terrain. He accompanied the patient and the party to the road at Pinkham Notch, arriving at 9:30 p.m. by headlamp.

ANALYSIS

The team of three was using the wrong equipment for a trip above treeline in the Presidential Range, where summer hiking trails turn into mountaineering routes in the winter. In these conditions, full crampons with strap-on or cuff bindings offer much better security; many brands work reasonably well even when attached to inappropriately soft and uninsulated boots. Microspikes-style devices are great for snow-packed low-angled trails under 15° to 20° in steepness, but the rubber straps stretch and come loose on steeper terrain, and the short points do not penetrate snow to grip the firm surface beneath.

On January 9, in a similar incident to the one analyzed at right, two winter climbers with Microspikes-style traction devices and no ice axes tumbled about 500 feet down the headwall of Tuckerman Ravine. One landed on a snow ledge (circled); the other continued to the bottom. Amazingly, neither was seriously injured. *Mount Washington Avalanche Center*

Three other winter climbers suffered long falls on Mt. Washington in early 2021 while using Microspikes-style traction devices instead of crampons. Long sliding falls kill more people in the Presidential Range than hypothermia or avalanches. Invest in stiff-soled mountaineering boots and crampons, and get proper training for self-arrest with an ice axe. (*Source: Mount Washington Avalanche Center.*)

FALLING ICE | Poor Position
Rumney

In midafternoon on March 12, a female climber (21) was hit by falling ice at the right end of the Parking Lot Wall at Rumney Rocks. She was standing at the base of the 75-foot-high Meadow Flows ice climb (WI3+) when a piece of ice naturally fell from an upper section of the climb. She was hit and reportedly knocked unconscious. Members of her climbing party assisted her and called 911. Other climbers were able to retrieve a Stokes litter stored about 100 yards away in the Parking Lot area.

Rumney Fire Department rescue personnel, with mutual aid of the Wentworth Fire Department, quickly responded to the 911 call. They contacted Dartmouth Hitchcock Advanced Response Team (DHART) for assistance, with an initial report of an unconscious person and possible head injury. Rescue personnel reached the injured within about 15 minutes, at which time she had been placed into the litter and regained consciousness. She was further stabilized, with preliminary assessment of broken ribs and back injuries. The litter was carried about 150 yards to an improvised helicopter landing zone in the campground meadow across the road from the incident site. She was flown to the DHART hospital facilities in Hanover, New Hampshire.

ANALYSIS

In any ice climbing location, icefall is a constant hazard. At the time of the incident, the air temperature was in the mid-40s (F) and the ice was in the sun. In this incident, the climber was a novice and may not have been aware she was standing in a hazard zone. Always seek sheltered positions when traversing, standing, or belaying below ice formations. Be extra cautious below steep walls, discontinuous ice, and ice curtains. If you are responsible for novices, make sure they appreciate this hazard as well.

The climber was fortunate the incident occurred close to a road, with a litter nearby, and was quickly accessible to rescue personnel. It is not known if she was wearing a helmet. (*Sources: Chief David Coursey, Rumney Fire Department, and the Editors.*)

FALL ON ROCK | Inadequate Protection
North Conway, Whitehorse Ledge, The Slabs

On October 5, two guides, Ryan McGuire (37) and Ryan Tilley (26), started up Sliding Board (5.7), a classic eight-pitch route on the Whitehorse Slabs, as a practice climb. On the fifth pitch (5.6), which follows a faint dike feature, McGuire had led about ten feet out from Tilley's belay when he felt himself slipping. He had not placed any gear above the anchor, and he fell about ten to fifteen feet below Tilley's belay. McGuire had broken his left arm and his right finger, which was bleeding badly.

A little before noon, Tilley called 911 and then started a self-rescue. He rappelled with McGuire while New Hampshire Fish and Game and volunteers from the New Hampshire Mountain Rescue Service responded below, along with a second party of AMGA guides who had been climbing an adjacent route. McGuire and Tilley reached the ground without further incident, with minor assistance.

ANALYSIS

On moderate, hard-to-protect terrain—which guides encounter often—solid movement skills form the basis of safety. Often the best protection is simply not falling off. Especially for guides, who often climb the same route repeatedly, it is easy to become complacent. McGuire wishes he had placed a few pieces past the belay, but is unsure if the terrain would have allowed much more protection. He stressed that he made a good decision by climbing with a partner well-versed in rock rescue. Had Tilley not acted quickly and competently, it would have taken them much longer to reach the ground and medical services. (*Source: The Editors.*)

NEW MEXICO

GROUND FALL | Nut Placement in Loose Rock
Truth or Consequences Area, Percha Creek

I, Jessica Hans (female, 33), had a significant ground fall on Barber Shop Cafe (5.8+) at Percha Creek in November. I ascended 15 to 20 feet and placed a number 5 Black Diamond Stopper in the roof section as my first piece of pro. I continued up another foot and then felt uneasy about the moves beyond the roof. I downclimbed back to the nut, which I thought was a bombproof placement, and had my partner (male, 33) take, so I could assess my next moves.

Upon weighting the nut, the entire rock came loose and blew out from the wall. I fell along with a watermelon-size boulder and my gear. I fell approximately ten feet, hit a ledge, fell a further five to ten feet, and landed sideways on my left ankle.

I was in shock for five to ten minutes. My partner and I deliberated calling SAR for assistance, but after assessing my injury we determined the ankle was the only really damaged area, and I was able to hop on one foot to get out of the creek area. I went to the emergency department in Las Cruces immediately, where they found nothing broken, and although the sprain was significant, there were no tears in ligaments or tendons. I was in a boot for one and a half months, then a brace. Mobility has improved considerably, and I was back on rock (leading sport, but no trad yet) after three months. (*Source: Jessica Hans.*)

ANALYSIS

Loose rock is a hazard in almost all climbing areas. Hans says, "Ultimately, I believe the accident happened because of a poor placement in loose rock. As much as I had tested the quality of the rock before placing the gear, I didn't count on hidden fissures in that feature."

While it's true that the immediate cause of this accident was the rock breaking and the gear pulling out, placing another piece of gear below the nut might have prevented the ground fall. An informal rule in trad climbing states: Always have two pieces between you and the hospital. Furthermore, a nut is not a multi-directional piece of gear; therefore, a cam is often advisable to use as a first piece. (*Source: The Editors.*)

NEW YORK

FALLING ROCK | Severed Rope
Shawangunks, The Trapps

On April 18, Gabe Schwartz (39) and Kile Simpson (33) were climbing Wrist, a two-pitch 5.6 in the Trapps area. Simpson, a climber with four years of experience, was leading the first pitch. Schwartz, who had been climbing for over ten years, wrote, "He (Kile) was nearing the top of the first pitch when he let out a yell." Schwartz assumed a fall had taken place. He "...took a step back to prepare for a big catch and looked up to see a large rock falling down the wall."

The rock landed at the bottom of the cliff and obliterated a dead tree before joining a scree field. At this point, Schwartz saw the lead rope lying limp on the ground. It had been severed about 40 feet below Simpson.

Schwartz recounts, "Once I notified him of the situation, he placed two cams and anchored off of them. He was at a hands-free stance. I happened to have my [own] rope with me, so I had a climber in the area belay me as I led up to the top of the first pitch. I set an anchor and tossed my partner the end of the rope so that he could tie in [and climb to my stance]. We finished the second pitch and retrieved all of our gear as we rappelled. We found the rock after the fact and estimated it to be 80 to 90 pounds.

ANALYSIS

Simpson wrote, "I was on an obvious line, but apparently off route. The rock that sheared seemed stable. I used it as a handhold. The rock sheared when I moved up after placing a cam. I then went direct into the cam. Having four points of contact and a large ledge was why I did not fall. I was not aware of the loose rock until after the incident." He was 100 feet up when the rope was severed, and he was fortunate that the weight of the block impacting his rope did not pull him off.

Kile Simpson holding the rock that cut his rope while he was leading. [Inset] The severed rope. *Gabe Schwartz (both photos)*

This accident resulted in a combination of the leader taking a less frequented line and possibly the presence of loose rock in the early spring due to the freeze/thaw cycle. Simpson was wearing a helmet. Schwartz cannot recall if he had his helmet on while belaying, but his rule was to wear a helmet 100 percent of the time while climbing and perhaps 50 percent of the time on the ground. Now, he always wears a helmet while belaying. (*Source: Gabe Schwartz.*)

LOOSE ROCK CRUSHES LEADER'S FOOT
Shawangunks, The Trapps

On March 23, a male climber (43) was climbing pitch two of Middle Earth (3 pitches, 5.6) when he apparently dislodged a large block that narrowly missed his partner, who was belaying atop the first pitch. In the process, the leader's left foot was crushed by another loose block.

The climber managed to continue to the top of pitch two and belayed from a tree. He brought his partner up and then rappelled to the base, keeping his weight on his good right foot. He later said, "I did not want to endanger any other climbers or rescuers trying to get to me." Once he was at the base, a rescue team ushered him down the trail and onto a ranger truck, after which an ambulance and then helicopter evacuated him to Westchester Medical Center. The climber lost all the toes of his left foot.

ANALYSIS

Loose rock is always a hazard, even on an area classic like Middle Earth. Climbers should test any potentially loose blocks by rapping on them and listening and watching for signs of movement. This climber was fortunate to have a steadfast partner who calmly assisted in the self-rescue and evacuation. He later posted a note on Mountain Project to avoid the route until rangers had the opportunity to assess and manage the issue—a thoughtful warning to fellow climbers. Similarly, climbers can mark wiggling blocks with a chalk X to warn other climbers until the loose rock can be removed. (*Sources: Mountain Project and the Editors.*)

FREE SOLO FALL
Shawangunks, The Trapps

On September 6, Stephen M. Buda III (56) was killed when he fell from 150 feet up Easy Street, a two-pitch 5.6. He was free soloing when he fell.

According to the Ulster County Sheriff's Office investigation, which included eyewitness accounts, Buda was climbing alone and had "ascended about 150 to 175 feet of the approximately 200-foot section of the climb when he fell." He was pronounced dead at the scene at about 5:30 p.m., deputies said.

ANALYSIS
Buda was a fireman and a very experienced climber. Park rangers and eyewitnesses said Buda slipped at the awkward crux of the route 150 feet up. According to Mountain Project, pitch two (the approximate point at which Buda might have fallen) starts with a "weird/ awkward move" and then traverses on terrain described at times to be "wet and slippery— one of those 'big hands, no feet' traverses." (*Sources: Connecticut Post, Mountain Project.*)

NORTH CAROLINA

FATAL FALL FROM ANCHOR | Inexperience at Cleaning
Pilot Mountain State Park, Parking Lot Area

During the late afternoon on August 23, Miriam Cho (30) and her partner Lawrence Quinnett were climbing the route Chicken Bone (5.6), located in the Parking Lot climbing area of Pilot Mountain State Park. Miriam led the climb and reached the anchors, where she began the task of cleaning the gear in preparation for lowering.

This was the first time Miriam had attempted to complete this transition, and Lawrence stated that he had coached her on the ground on how to clean an anchor safely. Lawrence noted that Miriam spent more time at the top anchors than a more experienced climber would have. She pulled up on the rope multiple times to take her weight off the rope or her personal anchor system (PAS). When she sat back as if ready to lower, she fell approximately 90 feet to the ground, her rope falling with her.

She received multiple fractures and other injuries in the fall. First responders stated she was breathing but not responsive. Her helmet was removed to check her pulse, and she was left in the position where she landed until she stopped breathing. At this point she was repositioned and CPR was started. Once paramedics arrived, they determined there was no heart activity and stopped CPR. (*Source: Ranger Nicholas Bowman.*)

ANALYSIS
It is believed Miriam used a PAS to tether herself to the anchors. She was found with a figure-of-eight on a bight attached to her belay loop with a locking carabiner and had untied from her figure eight follow-through tie-in knot. This suggests she intended to push a bight of the rope through the anchor and then tie a figure eight in the bight to clip to her belay loop. However, she apparently failed to pass the bight of rope through the rings first.

There are a few steps climbers can take to avoid a repeat of this tragic event. First, there should be clear communication between climber and belayer as to what's going to happen at the anchor before the climber leaves the ground. Second, new climbers can practice threading and cleaning a mock anchor on the ground before doing it at the top of a route. Once the climber is at the anchor, if communication is clear, the experienced belayer should verbally talk the climber through the steps of cleaning the anchor, or the climber can verbalize each step to the belayer for confirmation. And finally, once threaded through the anchor, the climber should make sure they are still on belay before committing to the rope. Have the belayer take the rope tight to confirm the system is working *before* unclipping the PAS or other tether from the anchor. (*Source: The Editors.*)

LONG LEADER FALL | Protection Pulled Out
Pisgah National Forest, Looking Glass Rock

Early in the afternoon on January 14, Forrest Lin (28) and Catherine Chee (28) began climbing The Nose (4 pitches, 5.8) on Looking Glass Rock. Both climbers reached the top of the 110-foot first pitch. Once the anchor and belay were established, Lin took the lead. The 90-foot second pitch moves right off the belay and follows a quartz dike to a bolted belay.

Lin described what happened next: "I became unintentionally off route and...tried to make my way back to the intended route, but the protection below was suspect. I got to a point where there was not very good protection about two feet below the dike. Here, I had placed a Black Diamond C4 cam (0.75) about knee height, but I knew it was not an ideal placement as I had only three lobes engaged. I stalled and thought through what I was going to do and decided to reach for the next hold. Unfortunately, I fell. The BD .75 popped and I continued to fall. As momentum continued to carry me, the next piece, a number 3 C4, came out. [The next piece], a nut I placed, ended up catching my fall."

Lin fell approximately 100 feet. During his fall, he tumbled a couple of times and in the process struck his head, damaging his helmet. "Catherine was able to arrest my fall and immediately called my name, but I was unable to respond. After approximately five minutes of contemplating our situation, she decided I needed medical attention after noticing blood coming from a lacerated ear. Thankfully, she had cell service and made the call to search and rescue. Because she knew our exact location, rescue personnel were able to reach us in approximately 60 minutes."

One of the first to arrive on the scene was Karsten Delap, a local guide and Transylvania County Rescue Squad member. He was able to climb to Lin and found him conscious. He secured and stabilized Lin and did a primary survey. During the survey, Delap noted a lacerated left ear, bloody nose, and a possible head injury. Delap was able to tandem-rappel with Lin to the ground. Transylvania Rescue Squad members were notified and requested the Mountain Area Medical Airlift helicopter (MAMA) for transport to Mission Memorial Hospital in Asheville.

Once rescuers arrived to aid Lin, Delap ascended to Chee and tandem-rappelled with her to the ground, where she was treated for mild hypothermia.

Looking Glass Rock. The unusual horizontal wrinkles called "eyebrows" create unique climbing and protection placements. The Nose is on the left side of the cliff (center of photo). *Karsten Delap*

ANALYSIS

Lin commented:

(1) *Guidebook:* I own two North Carolina guidebooks and researched the route, and truly thought I was going the intended way. Unfortunately, once I realized I was off route, it became incredibly difficult to get back on track.

(2) *Weather:* The day that we went climbing, there was still some snow on the ground from snowfall earlier in the week. That day in particular was also relatively cold (mid-40s F), and it is reasonable to think that in the darker parts of the wall with no sunlight that it was slicker than normal.

(3) *Gear Placement:* This goes along with the first item: Because I was a little off route, the gear placement was less than ideal, with suspect rock. (*Source: The Editors.*)

SWINGING LEADER FALL

Rumbling Bald, Comatose Area

Early afternoon on November 14, K. Tumek (31) and his wife were climbing the route Comatose (100', 5.8 trad) with K. leading. Somewhere on the climb he fell approximately 20 feet and swung into the rock face, injuring his hip and elbow. He was lowered to the ground by his wife. He was wearing a helmet.

The climber was unable to stand or walk out, due to his injury. Local rescuers arrived on the scene a short time later. K. was placed on a backboard and Stokes basket, carried a short distance, loaded into a UTV, driven to the trailhead, and finally transported to Rutherford Hospital. (*Source: From a report by park superintendent James Leatherwood.*)

ANALYSIS

When leading trad routes, climbers should not only focus their attention on route-finding and secure gear placements, but also assess the trajectory and consequences of a potential fall (the "what if" question). If a fall might result in a swing into a corner or other feature, additional protection or other steps may be required. (*Source: The Editors.*)

OREGON

FATAL FALL
Mt. Hood

On Sunday, May 30, a climber (male, 63) fell 500 feet from the Old Chute route on Mt. Hood (11,239 feet). He was descending the route with his adult son. He fell from around the 10,500-foot level—the steepest section of the climb.

Witnesses called 911 and the Clackamas County Sheriff's Office SAR team immediately responded, setting up a command post at Timberline Lodge and requesting assistance from Portland Mountain Rescue (PMR), the Hood River Crag Rats, and American Medical Response's Reach and Treat Team (AMR). A member of PMR and a member of the Crag Rats happened to be recreating on Mt. Hood when they learned of the accident. They immediately started toward the accident scene to assist with rescue efforts.

Around 10:30 a.m., rescuers made visual contact with the fallen climber, who was not moving. They found him deceased. The climber was loaded onto a skiable rescue litter basket, and at 4:20 p.m. they began making their way down the mountain.

ANALYSIS
While climbing mountains is inherently risky, no explanation of the events leading to this accident has been provided. It was an exceptionally busy weekend on Mt. Hood, and Portland Mountain Rescue offered a safety message for those climbing the mountain: "Warm weather at this time of year can create very unstable conditions on this area of Mt. Hood, including falling ice. The addition of many climbers of varying skill levels can add additional hazards. Exercise caution." (*Source: Clackamas County Sheriff's Office Public Information Unit.*)

STRANDED | Climbing Alone
Cascades, South Sister

On the morning of April 12, a climber (49) was soloing the North Face Couloir of South Sister (10,358 feet) in very thin conditions. He became stranded after climbing into an area with overhanging rocks above, having passed through terrain he was unable or unwilling to downclimb.

Fortunately, the climber was able to access his cell phone and call 911, despite poor cellular reception in the area. The call was made at 8:51 a.m. For several reasons, it took Deschutes County Sheriff's Office Search and Rescue about 6.5 hours to make hands-on contact with the soloist, largely due to the great difficulty in locating his position on the mountain. Despite three flights, visual confirmation via helicopter of his exact location was unsuccessful. Similarly, verbal contact once three SAR members were on scene was difficult due to the mountain's topography and weather. Since the climber had carried no rope or protection, he could not anchor himself during this extended search.

The climber eventually was located when three volunteer rescuers were dropped off at the South Sister summit and then downclimbed about 600 feet and traversed

Rescuers downclimbed from the summit of South Sister to reach a point above a climber who had been stranded for more than seven hours (yellow dot), rappelled to his position, fitted him with a harness, and then guided him to the summit. *Deschutes County Sheriff's Office*

about 500 feet eastward to be directly above the climber. Finally, at about 3:30 p.m., the climber was located. One of the volunteer rescuers rappelled to him, carefully fitted the climber with a harness, and connected him to a rope. Both the patient and rescuer then ascended to the belay. Within an hour, the subject was hoisted off the mountain via National Guard Blackhawk helicopter, with no known injuries aside from exhaustion and near hypothermia.

ANALYSIS

Although this route can be a moderate snow climb in good conditions, it did not have good snow coverage in mid-April, and the climber appears to have gotten off the best line in the steepest section.

Solo climbing is not only potentially dangerous to the climber, but also may be dangerous for bystanders and rescuers. The rescue operation was a huge resource drain and posed significant risk for the rescuers. The Deschutes County Sheriff's Office Search and Rescue team engaged 17 personnel for nearly 14 hours to safely extricate the climber. Multiple helicopter flights were needed for the search, to transport responders and equipment to the summit, and to hoist the subject off the mountain. The subject had not notified anyone of his objective, and he carried no gear with which to descend or anchor himself. (*Source: Caleb Bryce, Deschutes County Sheriff's Office Search and Rescue.*)

ASCENDING ERROR | System Failure
Central Oregon, Steelhead Falls

On September 17, at approximately 7 p.m., a Corvallis Mountain Rescue Unit (CMRU) member fell approximately 40 to 50 feet on high-angle rock while ascending a single rope. The accident took place during a training event at Steelhead Falls. The ground and rock were dry, with air temperature estimated to be in the high 70s F.

While ascending the rope, the subject's glove got caught on the exposed teeth of an Edelrid Spoc progress-capture pulley being used for ascension, while the climber was attempting to move it upward on the rope. As a result, the teeth of the progress-capture pulley failed to engage the rope and the pulley slid down the rope onto the subject's lower rope grab [*the term for any device or hitch that travels on the rope and automatically engages to arrest a fall*]. The lower rope grab consisted of a 5mm accessory cord configured as a foot loop and attached to the rope with a prusik hitch. This lower rope grab was connected to the subject's harness by a locking carabiner connected to an older model Metolius Ultimate Daisy Chain girth-hitched to their harness belay loop. The pulley collapsed and tended the prusik hitch (prevented the prusik from grabbing the rope) as it was weighted, resulting in loss of positive connection to the rope. The result was an uncontrolled fall to the ground.

The team member sustained only minor injuries, despite the significant mechanism of injury involved. Injuries were limited to abrasion and mild pain to the pelvis/back region. Other CMRU members at the scene performed an in-line traveling haul rescue to get the injured member back up to safety at the top of the cliff. [*Editor's Note: The use of the Edelirid Spoc above a prusik is not shown in the manufacturer's instructions.*]

ANALYSIS

The upper rope grab was defeated, fell down onto the lower rope grab (three-wrap prusik with 5mm accessory cord), and caused it to fail. A CMRU member was later able to re-create the cause of the accident using several combinations of progress-capture pulleys of various brands over friction hitches. It appears the cause of this accident was not directly associated with any particular brand of gear or type of friction hitch used, but rather the configuration of a "hard" rope grab over a "soft" rope grab.

A secondary cause of this incident was the climber's glove getting caught on the teeth of the upper ascender while manipulating the device, which may have prevented it from fully engaging the rope. The ascender was a pulley that was capable of overriding the prusik and breaking the friction grip of the hitch. One foot

When the climber's glove caught in the teeth of the progress-capture pulley, the device slid down the rope, causing the prusik hitch below to fail. The climber fell to the ground, suffering friction burns through the glove. *Joe McCormick, CMRU*

was on a ledge, partially supporting the climber's weight, and this may have made it harder to detect the initiation of the defeat of the upper ascender. By being only partially weighted (with some of the climber's weight being supported by the foot on a ledge) the grip of the lower prusik hitch may not have been solidly set and may have been looser around the rope than normal, allowing it to be broken more easily.

Other contributing factors:

- Inexperienced climber using newly learned skills with high-angle exposure on rock while ascending a rope
- Lack of full familiarity with all components used in the ascending system
- Improvised activity, informal environment (prior to start of "real" training agenda)
- Expert halo effect possibly obfuscated or minimized the hazards of the activity
- Fatigue near the end of the day, after a long drive to training site by the climber

(*Source: Joe McCormick, Corvallis Mountain Rescue Unit.*)

FALL ON ROCK
Smith Rock State Park, The Dihedrals

On November 28, two experienced climbers impacted each other when the lead climber fell off Darkness at Noon (5.13b). He pulled his belayer (42) into him, and the collision resulted in several neck and back compression fractures to the belayer.

A SAR volunteer who was hiking in the area at the time of the accident called for help. The call went in at 11:10 a.m., and the SAR team was hands-on with the patient by 12:36 p.m. They assessed injuries and transported the climber to higher-level care.

ANALYSIS
It's not uncommon for a belayer to be pulled off their feet and even strike the wall when catching a falling leader (see page 55). In this case, the belayer was pulled significantly upward because the leader was more than 100 pounds heavier. The pair had reportedly climbed together for years, including many catches of the heavier male by the lighter female. It is not known what made this particular catch so much more significant.

One can assume that it was a long fall or that the belayer was positioned in such a way that the forces generated pulled her violently upward. [*Editor's Note: A tool specifically designed to address this situation is the Edelrid Ohm, which is clipped to the first bolt and mitigates the forces generated by a leader that is much heavier than the belayer.*] The belayer was not wearing a helmet.

The fact that the patient was wearing a climbing harness made maintaining spinal precautions while repositioning the patient into the litter for transport much easier. As a side note, SAR was initially requested only to assist in walking the injured climber to her car, when she in fact had life-threatening spinal injuries. (*Source: Caleb Bryce, Deschutes County Sheriff's Office Search and Rescue.*)

TEXAS

FALL ON ROCK | Inexperience
San Antonio, Buddha Belly Wall

On January 9, a man approximately 21 to 25 years old fell on Fear of Falling (5.11b) and broke both ankles. According to three witnesses who posted on Mountain Project, the man and his partner—a female approximately 21 years old—appeared completely inexperienced. The pair ignored the multiple warnings from experienced climbers regarding back-clipping and improper belaying. At one point, the young man's harness slipped below his waist with the leg loops hanging below his knees.

Ryan Thornton was climbing a route near the pair. He wrote, "I saw the couple approach the wall from the trail. I remember overhearing the young woman say they had traveled from Houston to climb." (This crag was open while most in Texas were closed due to COVID.) "I noticed all their gear, particularly the rope and draws, looked shiny and new. Neither was wearing helmets. When they showed up they set up one of those inflatable couch things not far from where they would be belaying. At the risk of sounding rude, we knew immediately that these two had no business being there. They just looked like kids who bought some climbing gear.

"The young man started making his way up Fear of Falling. He was obviously having trouble. He started making his way past the first bolt but wasn't having much luck. He kept awkwardly getting above the bolt, then holding the draw and swinging back down. I remember hearing him say, 'Okay, I'm going to try this one more time, and if I can't get it I'm going to come back down.' His partner said, 'Okay.'

"My partner nudged me and pointed out how much slack the young woman was pulling through the Grigri. The guy was 20 to 30 feet up, and the woman had so much slack out, it piled at her feet. My partner and I looked at each other with an 'I can't watch this' expression. Almost immediately, the guy peeled off the wall upside down. With the slack, he fell almost to the ground.

"His belayer is frozen, just holding the rope and Grigri," Thornton wrote. "Luckily, another climbing party of three or four guys came over, got him right side up, and then helped lower him to the ground."

It was later reported on Mountain Project that the fallen climber's belayer was seeking directions to a nearby sports store to buy a dolly with which to cart the victim to the hospital. He had apparently broken both ankles.

ANALYSIS
Climbing is dangerous and rewards foolhardy bravado or naivete with injury, or worse. The post on Mountain Project generated comments regarding intervention of unsafe practices. Opinions, as always ran the gamut, but the bottom line was that the pair ignored or failed to understand multiple warnings before the belayer became agitated. It appears that, short of physical intervention (improbable given that the leader was leading and belayer belaying), the other climbers did what they could do. (Sources: Ryan Thornton, Mountain Project.)

Editor's Note: "Essentials: Speak Up!" in ANAC 2019 proposes ways to intervene when climbers observe potentially dangerous behavior.

UTAH

TWO CLIMBERS FALL WHILE SIMUL-CLIMBING
House Range, Notch Peak

On November 2, three climbers were linking the lower north face with the upper north face of remote Notch Peak. They completed the lower face via Western Hardman (12 pitches, 5.10c). They then started up the upper face on Book of Saturday (12 pitches, 5.11a R).

Climber A was leading and linking pitches on two 8.5mm, 60m half-ropes. He was clipping alternately. He passed the bolt anchor at the end of pitch three, and as he neared the anchor for pitch four, Climber B—who was clipped to pitch two's belay anchor—shortened his tie-in by 15 feet. Climber C, the belayer, took A off belay on that strand of rope, and B began simul-climbing. Meanwhile, Climber C continued belay-

The impressive north face of Notch Peak in western Utah, with the 1,500-foot upper tier in the background. Book of Saturday, where this incident occurred, climbs the left side of the face. The climber is atop the lower tier; the Western Hardman route finishes behind him. *Derek DeBruin*

ing A with the remaining length of the other strand.

Shortly after beginning pitch three, Climber B lost his balance and lunged for a hold. The hold broke and he fell, dragging A down with him.

Climber A was six feet above a bolt—his last piece of protection—when he was pulled off. There was no progress-capture device on the last piece. [*Editor's Note: When the rope runs through a progress-capture device that is clipped to protection, a simul-climbing lead climber is prevented from getting pulled downward if the follower falls.*] Climber A flipped upside down during a 30- to 40-foot fall. At the same time, B fell 30 feet, plunging past the pitch two belay and in the process spraining his ankle. He ended up hanging in free space. Climber A struck his heels, back, and head during the fall but remained conscious. He was lowered to the (intermediate) pitch three anchor. Climber B managed to pull in and clip directly into a bolt from the previous pitch and was belayed on a Munter hitch to the belay anchor by C. The group self-rescued by rappelling the route and reversing the long approach back to the car.

ANALYSIS

Simul-climbing can make the difference in completing a long route, as it often allows the team to move faster and forgo time-consuming belay transitions. The disadvantages include an increased fall risk for all involved—this accident is a prime example. While this team was very experienced, several factors came into play. Lunging for a loose hold initiated the falls, and the absence of a progress-capture device on the last bolt guaranteed a long plunge for Climber A. The team's choice to use 8.5mm ropes was a measure of their goal of efficiency. In this case it elevated the risk, as the rope that caught the two falling climbers snagged on the rock, tearing the sheath open and revealing the rope's core.

Though Mountain Project says this route has "the commitment of a long wall or alpine route and the seriousness of hard, sand-in-your-eye desert routes or adventure routes in the Black Canyon," that doesn't mean unnecessary risks are required. Climber A says that linking pitches "wasn't necessary—there was time to stop and pitch it out." He also adds, "It was one of those worst things that could happen in a worst-place scenario." (*Sources: Climber A and Mountain Project.*)

SLIDE ON SNOW | Inadequate Equipment
Wasatch Range, Mt. Olympus

James Roache (54) died after sliding 100 feet on snow before falling into a rocky moat on Mt. Olympus on May 22. He was preparing to climb the popular West Slabs (5.5). This long, moderate rock climb lies at relatively high elevation and often holds snow at the base in early season. Roache and his climbing partner were near the base of the route when he slipped on steep snow and fell into the moat, the narrow space between the deep snow and a rock wall. The Salt Lake County Sheriff's Search and Rescue team responded and recovered his body the same day.

ANALYSIS
Tragically, we reported a nearly identical incident in ANAC 2020 (page 95). Fortunately, that person survived. The West Slabs of Olympus see lots of traffic. The climbing is easy, but the peak holds serious hazards for the unprepared, including lingering snow at the base that leads to falls on approaches and sometimes descents. Roache was very experienced, having climbed Aconcagua, Denali, and Kilimanjaro. However, the night before it had rained and frozen on top of the snowy trail leading up to the climbing area, and he wasn't carrying an ice axe. (*Sources: www.thenewstribune.com and the Editors.*)

LOOSE ROCK
Little Cottonwood Canyon, Gate Buttress

On Sunday, October 10, Mason Boos (25) and two companions were climbing in the Gate Buttress area. At about 1:15 p.m., Boos was unroped and traversing 3rd-class terrain below Satan's Corner (5.8) to reach the start of Half-A-Finger (5.9+). He pulled on a large block, reported to be the size of a Subaru. The block dislodged, causing him to fall 20 to 30 feet. "After he hit the ground, the boulder he had pulled out fell on top of him before continuing to roll down the mountain," said Sgt. Melody Cutler of Greater Salt Lake's Unified Police Department. The boulder nearly hit two other climbers further below, though they escaped unscathed.

Boos' climbing partner was belaying another climber nearby and was able to quickly reach him, establish him in a stable position, and call emergency services. Boos was not breathing, and his partner began CPR. Other climbers set up fixed lines for EMS to access the scene quickly and safely. When EMS arrived shortly afterward, Boos had not been breathing unassisted for over 20 minutes and was pronounced dead.

ANALYSIS
Boos was very experienced and a well-known member of the Salt Lake climbing and skiing community. He was on familiar ground, having frequently climbed at

Gate Buttress. The traverse he fell from is a common route to scramble back and forth between two popular sub-areas within Gate Buttress: Beckey's Wall and the Dihedrals Area.

Loose rock is an ever-present hazard that can be difficult or impossible to fully mitigate. Best practices include wearing a helmet, testing holds, and using a rope and gear for protection when practical. [For more information, see Safer 4th Class, by Tico Gangulee, ANAC 2018.] Still, rapid unroped movement on 3rd-class terrain is often standard practice. Given that fact, it is imperative to remain vigilant for loose rock even in heavy-use areas such as Little Cottonwood Canyon. (Sources: Salt Lake County Search and Rescue, News Reports, and Climbing Magazine.)

RAPPEL FAILURE | Dropped Rope
Castle Valley, Castleton Tower

On February 6, Clarissa Fortier (29) and Ariel* (32) climbed the Kor-Ingalls Route (4 pitches, 5.9+) on Castleton Tower. Ariel was an Israeli living in the United States, and Fortier was an American with six years of climbing experience throughout Colorado and southeastern Utah. Fortier had climbed Kor-Ingalls twice previously.

The morning forecast was good for the south-facing Kor-Ingalls: highs in the 40s F, sunny, and no wind advisory, according to Fortier. The team discussed rappel options and decided on a single 70-meter rope to descend the north face rappel route. On pitch two, they considered bailing due to cold and high winds. They chose to continue, as the climbing was well within their abilities and they had sufficient clothing. They summited at 2:30 p.m. in high winds and were eager to descend. Ariel got to the rappel station and began untangling the rope.

At that point, the pair had a miscommunication. Fortier, having experienced stuck rappel ropes on other desert routes, suggested saddlebagging the ropes due to the high winds. Ariel, eager to descend, proceeded to set up the rappel and threw one side of the rope down before locating the middle mark. This particular rappel station had larger than typical rap rings. After failing to locate the middle mark, Ariel took the other end–shorter in length than the side that had already been tossed–and released it. At that point the longer end was picked up by the wind and sucked through the anchor. The climbers had tied knots in both ends of the rope, but the stopper knot was pulled through the large rappel rings. The two climbers found themselves rope-less on top of the 400-foot tower.

Fortier recounts, "We had a phone and an LTE signal, so we called a friend in Moab." After waiting in vain for a party they'd seen below and realizing their friends would not reach the base until dark, Fortier was encouraged by friends to call Grand County police around 3:30 p.m.

With the wind gusting over 50 mph, a helicopter circled the tower, eventually landing on the summit around 5 p.m. to drop two rescuers. The two rescuers waited atop Castleton while the climbers were helicoptered to a spot about a mile from the Castleton parking lot. They were driven to the Castleton trailhead and then hiked back up to the base of the tower in their socks, as their approach shoes, climbing packs, and car keys were all at the base of the tower.

[*Not the climber's real name.]

ANALYSIS

Fortier says, "There are quite a few lessons to take away from this event. The greatest one: We should have secured a part of the rope to the anchor or to ourselves, because it is possible to drop the rope at the anchor station, especially in the high winds. She adds, "Another aspect of this event is that Ariel and I did not have clear communication, and I allowed the eagerness of getting off the tower to take precedent over my desire to rap using saddlebags. This event was a textbook example of how rushing can lead to situations that are unsafe. Thankfully, we got out of this situation safely, but I have a better understanding of how poor weather conditions, as well as fatigue and hunger, can cause key elements to go overlooked or get skipped altogether." (*Source: Clarissa Fortier.*)

Saddlebagging, shown here in the Wind River Range, is a useful technique for the first climber down to keep the ropes under control while rappelling in windy conditions. *Bjorn Rasmussen*

FALL ON ROCK | Inadequate Protection
Indian Creek, Cliffs of Insanity

On the afternoon of October 3, I (Ryan McAvoy, age 24) fell about 50 feet from a route called Vinciny (5.10). The route is 60 feet tall.

It was our second day in the Creek, and I was climbing with a mix of old and new friends. I agreed to lead Vinciny. It starts out fingers, turns to hands, then gains a ledge before a final flake to the anchors. My phone was dead and I'm not sure if we had a guidebook, but I talked with a new friend, Peggy, who had climbed the route before. I brought the gear I thought I would need.

I am relatively new to leading trad climbs. However, in the months leading up to climbing Vinciny, I had been leading multi-pitch routes in Big and Little Cottonwood canyons. I had just returned from a trip to Yosemite. I was feeling good about my abilities.

The first 45 feet was a little spicy and fun. I had placed a couple of finger-size cams in the first part. I then placed a number 2 and then a bomber number 3 Camalot before climbing onto a ledge. There was a flake to my left and a small crack to the right that went straight to the anchors, 15 feet above. I wanted to place something in the flake, but I hadn't brought any .75s. Peggy asked if I wanted to pull up some cams of that size, but I declined and ended up placing a purple Metolius TCU in the small crack. I laybacked up the flake, smearing my feet on a shallow left facing corner. It wasn't very secure, but I made good progress, running it out because I didn't have gear that would fit and placing would have been difficult.

I got to the bolt anchor but couldn't quite reach it due to awkward feet. I unclipped my personal anchor system so it would be easier to clip the anchor. I decided to reach the chains, grab them, and then clip myself in. As I was reaching for the chains, I fell.

On the way down, my right ankle hit the ledge. I flipped upside down for the rest of the fall. The purple TCU pulled, and luckily the bomber number 3 caught me. I was not far from the ground when I came to a stop. Peggy lowered me, and two others immediately came to see if I was alright. I believe the first thing I said was, "I think I'm okay." However, I realized my right ankle was not okay.

After immobilizing my ankle using Chaco sandals, jackets, and tape, I took some ibuprofen. We rigged up a few different ways to carry me, using harnesses, slings, and carabiners. A large group of people had assembled to help, and it took us about 1.5 to 2 hours to get back to the cars.

Editor's Note: Ryan was driven to the emergency room in Moab, where he was diagnosed with a dislocated ankle, fractured fibula, and fractured posterior malleolus. He has since recovered nearly fully.

ANALYSIS

I made several mistakes. The biggest and most impactful was I let myself become overconfident, even cocky. I felt good on the climbs I had done the day before and thought Vinciny would be within my abilities. This overconfidence played into complacency when I didn't seek out a guidebook or Mountain Project for better gear beta. The next huge mistake was choosing not to not haul up a 0.75 cam when I had the option. For some reason, I got it into my head that pulling up gear would mess with the "purity" of the onsight.

To add to the sketchiness of my situation, I was run-out on a purple TCU (the second-smallest in the range), not ideal for catching a big fall, and also not ideal for sandstone. Even if I had decent protection in the flake, there was still potential to deck on the ledge.

[*Editor's Note: While skipping a clip on an overhanging sport climb can be exhilarating, punching to the chains, sans gear on soft sandstone, can lead to injury, as Ryan can now attest.*]

Almost everyone on scene, including myself, had at least a WFR certification. This made evacuating me super smooth. I'm extremely grateful to my many first responders for making a bad situation as good as could be. For everything that went wrong that day, a lot of things went right. I'm lucky to be alive. (*Source: Ryan McAvoy.*)

LOOSE ROCK | Broken Leg
Zion National Park, Mt. Greer

On June 1, a father and son team experienced rockfall while attempting a first ascent variation on Mt. Greer, a 1,500-foot-tall formation in Zion National Park. While leading the final pitch, Aaron Davis (42) dislodged a large block. The rock struck his son, Ian (16), who was belaying, breaking the latter's femur. They called 911 and were rescued by helicopter.

The team was very experienced and chose an objective that was big, accessible, and near the west entrance of the park. This sector has cell service, and that was to play a role in their rescue.

The pair started climbing at dawn. After climbing three or four pitches of an existing route called Slow and Delirious, they continued straight up into new terrain. By 4 p.m. they had climbed seven new pitches up to 5.11- and were perhaps 100 feet from the summit. Above, an unclimbed chimney led to the top. In his haste to summit, Aaron placed the belay where debris from the chimney would funnel.

Halfway up the chimney, "The wall cut in a bit, like the backs of two offset books," Aaron recalled. "There was a perfect hand crack in back. I barely touched the outside edge with my left foot when a mini-fridge-sized block cut loose."

Ian Davis being plucked off Mt. Greer in Zion by a Utah Department of Public Safety helicopter. *Aaron Davis*

The rock severed the lead rope before striking Ian's leg. Still wedged in the chimney, Aaron placed a cam and rappelled with his tagline. A quick assessment revealed that Ian's femur was broken.

Aaron leaned out enough from the wall to get a cell signal and was connected with the Park Service. A Utah Department of Public Safety (DPS) helicopter showed up in three hours. A rescuer was lowered, and the climbers were plucked off one at a time.

ANALYSIS

Summit fever can cause climbers to rush and make poor choices. The position of the belay and hasty climbing, combined with the deteriorating sandstone quality toward the top of most Zion formations, led to the accident. Aaron recalled, "We should have identified the obvious natural hazards. There were options, but I was blind to them in the moment. Had we slowed down a bit, we would have moved our belay out of the shooting gallery and sent." (*Source: Aaron Davis.*)

WASHINGTON

ROCKFALL | Child Hit at Base of Cliff
Index Town Wall

On July 10, an unidentified climber (age unknown) released a rock while climbing. The rock fell and struck a child (age 6) on the head. The child was playing at the base of a route called Zoom (5.10d) and was not wearing a helmet. Snohomish County Fire District 26 responded, and the child was flown by helicopter to Seattle. After many months in the hospital and several surgeries, the youngster is alive and in ongoing therapy for the injury.

ANALYSIS
Overhead hazards at the crag pose risks to all. All bystanders at climbing crags will benefit from wearing a helmet. This includes children. Several climbing hardware companies make helmets for kids down to age three (or head circumference of 18.9 inches). In the past, a head injury from falling rock at a rock climbing crag might have been more unusual. This accident is the fourth of its kind we are reporting this year. As climbing grows in popularity and more climbers—and climbing families—flock to the crags, extra vigilance will need to become the norm. (*Sources: Seattle Herald and the Editors.*)

FALL ON ROCK
Index, Inner Walls

On the afternoon of July 20, I (male, 29) was climbing at Index with P, who had several years of climbing experience. P could comfortably lead 5.11 sport routes, but had limited experience with trad climbing. I had four years of mountaineering experience and 1.5 years of trad.

Having both warmed up, we moved toward a popular 100-foot trad climb, Toxic Shock (5.9), that I wanted to lead. I had successfully top-roped the route twice and felt I had a reasonable chance of success.

I climbed the first part of the route and reached a large ledge with an obvious horn. I then began the second part, placing two cams in relatively short succession to protect against ledge fall. I came to a hand crack and climbed this part as a layback, with my body positioned at an angle. This position (unnoticed by me) put a small ledge directly in my fall line. Approximately six feet above my last protection, I successfully placed a cam from the layback position. I pulled up rope and attempted to clip, but my feet, positioned in a smear on the protruding edge of the crack, slipped.

Due to the angle of my body, I rotated slightly, mainly facing outward as I fell. I contacted the small ledge with my left ribcage. The fall distance to the ledge was about eight to 12 feet. I continued to fall slightly further, and the two cams I had placed earlier held.

It was immediately obvious to me that I had broken at least one rib. My climbing partner lowered me, and I walked (in pain) to the car and drove myself to the hospital. The ER confirmed three broken ribs, with no other complications.

ANALYSIS

The main reason for this injury is I failed to place protection in a manner consistent with the ledge-fall hazard. My climbing mentors had continually bombarded me with warnings of being vigilant about ledges. As I departed the large ledge, this reminder was loud and clear. However, I failed to observe that I had climbed into a position above a second, smaller ledge.

A contributing factor may have been my climbing technique: Better climbers might choose to jam this section instead of laybacking, keeping the body more centered on the crack and making gear placements and clipping more manageable. [Editor's Note: Laybacking is more intuitive than harder-to-learn jamming skills. It is probably the way this climber originally top-roped the route. As he learned, laybacking generates a pump faster than jamming while often making placing, visually assessing, and clipping of gear, much harder.] Another contributing factor is that I was pulling up rope to clip when I fell, adding slack in the rope. (Source: Vinny Couming.)

FALL IN GYM | Impalement
Northern Washington Climbing Gym

On June 17, Brandon Frohbieter (34) was climbing unroped on an indoor wall about 12 feet off the floor. Although the route was equipped with an autobelay device, Frohbieter was not clipped to it. His plan was to check out the moves in order to decide if he wanted to climb the entire route using the autobelay.

Routesetting was being done in an adjacent area, and the routesetters had used plastic fencing to cordon off the area. A vertical PVC pipe, commonly seen in gyms, held up the plastic ribbon tape that comprised the fencing.

Frohbieter liked the moves and decided to jump down, clip into the autobelay, and do the climb to the top. He jumped and was impaled by the PVC pipe.

Frohbieter recalled, "I looked down my right shoulder, and I just saw the ground, so I just kind of dropped from the wall. I just landed down straight on that pipe. I started screaming at the top of my lungs.

"Up until the moment it happened, I was just expecting to hit the ground," Frohbieter said. "And I had no idea what happened. I just knew that I was in excruciating pain. And something terrible had happened. And I couldn't really feel my bottom half, and I knew blood was pooling around."

Plastic stanchion post similar to the type used to fence off areas for route-setting in gyms.

Frohbieter was taken to a nearby emergency room. His extensive injuries included a fractured sacrum, coccyx, tibial plateau, and burst T7 vertebra.

ANALYSIS

This improbable accident was met by some climbers with skepticism when Frohbieter initially posted the story at Mountain Project. Unfortunately, his accident and horrendous injuries were very much real. While climbing gyms are generally very safe, the unique aspects of our sport make any style or venue for ascent potentially dangerous. Situational awareness is beneficial even indoors. Despite his physical and financial distress, Frohbieter to his credit recognizes "the risk and the consequence" of climbing and has had only good things to say about the gym and its owner. (*Sources: Brandon Frohbieter, Climbing.com.*)

ACUTE MOUNTAIN SICKNESS
Mt Rainier, Disappointment Cleaver

On August 9, Climber 1 (60), Climber 2 (55), and five friends (ages 30 to 40+) from the Wasatch and Potomac Mountain clubs were attempting the Disappointment Cleaver route on Rainier. At 10,080 feet (Camp Muir), two members elected not to attempt the summit. The remaining five began ascending at 11 p.m. At about the 12,300-foot level, Climber 1 and Climber 2 reported feeling sick. After a rest break, Climber 2 felt even sicker.

When checked, Climber 2 was minimally responsive. He was immobile and seemed to be drifting in and out of consciousness. After a quick assessment, the climbing party prepared to report the climber's condition via inReach. At this point, several guided parties arrived. The guides performed a more complete assessment and radioed the National Park Service. After about 30 minutes, it was decided that two WFR-trained guides would stay with the patient (and the climbing team) and wait for additional help to arrive after dawn.

In the morning, Climber 2 was transported by helicopter long-line to Camp Muir. From there he was helicoptered down to Paradise at 5,400 feet and eventually transferred to the hospital in Puyallup. He had improved rapidly during the helicopter descent and was discharged from the hospital that night without a conclusive diagnosis. The climbing party's working assumption was a case of acute mountain sickness (AMS), lapsing into high altitude cerebral edema (HACE). Their conclusions were based on the nature of the symptoms and rapid improvement with descent.

ANALYSIS

The patient had eaten and drunk fluids normally at Camp Muir before the summit attempt. He had been to 10,000 feet regularly in the Wasatch Mountains without incident but had experienced AMS (though not with this sort of severity) on one occasion at 12,000 feet. Climbing Rainier on a typically fast visitor schedule poses acclimatization problems, since most trips to the mountain start near sea level. The climbing party stated that it would have been desirable to have experience at 13,000 to 14,000 feet prior to attempting Mt. Rainier. However, acute mountain sickness, high altitude pulmonary edema, and HACE can strike even experienced climbers and even at relatively low elevations (roughly 2,500 meters or 8,200 feet above sea level). (*Sources: Climber 1 and the Editors.*)

WEST VIRGINIA

TOP-ROPE SOLOING | Device Unclipped from Rope
New River Gorge, Lower Meadow

On November 30, Trevor Stuart (33), an expert climber with 10 years of experience, was solo top-roping The Greatest Show on Earth (5.13a) in the New River Gorge. After a fall, he became detached from his rope. He hit the ground after an estimated 60-foot fall. He was discovered by other climbers and evacuated. Stuart spent one week in the ICU with injuries including lacerations to his right arm and kidney, fractures of the thoracic and cervical spine, a subdural hematoma, and five broken ribs.

ANALYSIS
Stuart was using a Petzl Shunt with no backup device as a self-belay on a single 9.5mm dynamic rope. He'd used this particular system for at least a year, after seeing it demonstrated on a professional climber's YouTube video. On the day of the accident, he climbed with his rope weighted at the bottom with approach shoes and cams.

Stuart wrote in an email, "I'm certain the Shunt was set up properly since my routine involves weighting it before leaving the ground or taking myself off a midpoint anchor." His Shunt was undamaged and "still looks as good as new." He believes that the "Scorpion Catch," demonstrated on climbing guide Yann Camus' YouTube page, is the only explanation for the device detaching from his rope. [See page 48 for a similar incident in Colorado and more details on how the "Scorpion Catch" can cause this device to detach from a rope.] Petzl explicitly states that the Shunt is to be used only as a rappel backup and never should be used for self-belay. (Sources: Trevor Stuart, Climbing.com.)

WYOMING

FALL ON ROCK | Inadequate Protection
Grand Teton National Park, Disappointment Peak

On July 25, at 10:50 a.m., the Jenny Lake rangers received a report of an injured climber on Open Book (5.9) in Garnet Canyon. The reporting party told the ranger that Climber 1 (27) had taken a leader fall and had an open fracture to the left leg that was bleeding heavily, and the climber was potentially going into shock. The belayer was unable to lower the leader to the ground.

Based on subsequent investigation, Climber 1 had started up their second pitch, which began with an undercling and layback flake just above the belay. Climber 1 had placed a single piece of protection before falling. The protection pulled. Neither climber had clipped the lead rope to the anchor as a first piece of protection. Climber 2, who was belaying off his harness, had difficulty holding the fall. Climber 1 and Climber 2 had intermediate developed climbing skills.

Helicopter 35HX, with pilot Steve Wilson, flew a recon of the scene and landed two rangers in Garnet Meadows to start hiking to the base of the climb. The helicopter returned to the Lupine Meadows rescue cache at 11:45 a.m. and was rigged for short-haul. The pilot and spotter determined that a single rescuer could be safely inserted into the accident scene.

Once at the belay stance, the rescuer provided emergency medical care to stabilize Climber 1 and splinted the climber's legs for evacuation. The rescuer and Climber 1 were extracted by helicopter.

ANALYSIS

Open Book is a justifiably popular Teton classic. It also has some of the same hazards one would expect on a multipitch alpine rock climb, including tricky protection. In this case, placing an additional piece might have prevented such a long fall. Also, clipping the lead rope through a runner at the belay would have redirected the fall and made catching the fall easier. This is a standard practice among experienced trad climbers. (*Sources: Ranger Ken Kreis, Grand Teton National Park, and the Editors.*)

FALL ON ROCK | Climbing Unroped
Grand Teton National Park, Mt. Owen

The entrance to the Koven Couloir (A), seen from the Teton Glacier. When the couloir has melted out, as seen here in early August 2020, climbers must choose between the loose gully or technical rock to the left. The climbing is considerably easier on snow earlier in the summer. *Ryan Stolp*

At approximately 3:45 p.m. on August 12, the Jenny Lake rangers were notified by Climber 1 (age unknown) that his female climbing partner, Climber 2 (age 39), had sustained a 20- to 25-foot fall while ascending the lower couloir on the Koven Route. Climber 1 reported that Climber 2 had leg abrasions, back pain, and was unable to move.

Climbers 1 and 2 had been attempting to climb a slab to the left of the normal Koven Couloir start. Climber 2 was unroped at the time of the fall and was fortunate to stop without tumbling further. Climbers 1 and 2 stated they chose this line because the rock looked cleaner and involved less "dirt climbing" compared with the standard route. Climbers 1 and 2 had intermediate climbing skills.

Helicopter 35HX performed a reconnaissance flight with rangers Hunsaker and Heerdt on board and then landed on the Teton Glacier. Hunsaker and Heerdt left the helicopter and climbed to the scene, arriving at 5:10 p.m.

After a patient assessment, a request was made for one additional ranger, additional medical equipment, and a litter for a short-haul rescue. After receiving additional medical care, Climber 2 was packaged into a litter and short-hauled to the Lupine Meadows rescue cache and then transported to the hospital by park ambulance.

ANALYSIS
Big mountains can present an array of unforeseen difficulties, even on relatively moderate climbs with low technical grades. The Koven Route is usually rated around 5.4 with easy snow climbing. It is considerably easier in early season, when the lower couloir is filled with snow. The climbers' decision to avoid the melted-out couloir forced a second choice of whether to rope up and place protection on the rock climbing to the left of the couloir. Balancing the need for speed and desire for protection is always a difficult decision in the mountains; in this case, the climbers' choice led to a fall and a rescue. (*Sources: Ranger Ken Kreis, Grand Teton National Park, and the Editors.*)

STRANDED ON SUMMIT
Grand Teton National Park, Grand Teton

At 9 p.m. on August 30, the Jenny Lake rangers received a cell phone call from a climbing party of two requesting help getting down from the summit of the Grand Teton. The two climbers had left their camp at the Lower Saddle at 6 a.m. and spent 12 hours climbing the Lower Exum route (5.7), arriving at the Wall Street ledge at 6 p.m. They decided to continue climbing the Upper Exum, reaching the summit around 9 p.m. Climber 1 and Climber 2 had intermediate skills.

After a brief attempt to find the Owen-Spalding descent route, Climber 1 and Climber 2 concluded it was too dangerous for them to descend without help. One of the climbers called Teton Dispatch and described the predicament to ranger M. Shain. The climber indicated they were uninjured but would "likely die" if they tried to descend the icy rock route in the dark with only one headlamp. The climber also stated that neither of them had appropriate clothing to spend the night. With very little power left on the climber's cell phone, ranger Shain instructed the climbers to find a site protected from the wind and told them it would be many hours before any help could reach them. Shortly thereafter, the climber's phone battery died.

At 11 p.m., rangers N. Ronczkowski and C. Heerdt departed from the Lupine Meadows trailhead for the summit of the Grand Teton. They arrived at the NPS Lower Saddle camp at 2:15 a.m. on August 31 and added food, water, warm layers, climbing equipment, and crampons to their packs. The rangers continued up the Owen-Spalding route, reaching the summit of the Grand at 5 a.m. Shortly thereafter, the stranded party was found near the top of the Ford Couloir, to the southwest of the summit. The climbers were uninjured but very weak from their unplanned bivouac.

After receiving food, water, and warm clothing, Climbers 1 and 2 were short-roped down the upper Owen-Spalding route and assisted down the rappel to the Upper Saddle. At 7:25 a.m., ranger Ronczkowski reported that the rescued party was capable of continuing their descent to the Lower Saddle without any further assistance.

ANALYSIS
Late in the day it is easy to get overextended by the promise of a summit. One also has to account for the rigors of the descent after a long day. This party could have made the choice to descend along Wall Street in the evening after already spending 12 hours to complete the Lower Exum. Their decision to continue up another 1,000 vertical feet of easier but still technical terrain led to a cold night on the summit. On any long mountain route, sufficient water, food, extra clothing, and headlamps must be carried to allow either a safe nighttime descent or unplanned bivouac. (*Sources: Ranger Ken Kreis, Grand Teton National Park, and the Editors.*)

FALL ON ROCK | Off Route, Climbing Unroped
Grand Teton National Park, Teewinot

On September 4, the Jenny Lake rangers were notified that a climber had reported a deceased solo climber on the upper east face of Teewinot. Helicopter 35HX, with Steve Wilson as pilot and rangers on board, performed a reconnaissance flight. The deceased climber was seen at the base of the Black Chimney, north (climber's right) of the standard east face route. After returning to Lupine Meadows, rangers were short-hauled to the deceased climber's location, arriving on scene at 1:54 p.m. Rangers conducted an investigation of the scene and packaged the deceased climber for extraction.

The upper east side of Teewinot, showing the approximate line of (A) the standard east face route and (B) the general direction of the Black Chimney route. *David Goldstein*

The deceased climber was believed to have fallen approximately 50 to 100 feet. During the subsequent investigation, the climber was identified as a foreign national working in the United States and on a solo road trip. A map found in the climber's pack suggested the climber was attempting to climb the east face route. Other climbers reported seeing the individual the previous day beginning his ascent from Lupine Meadows at about 9:40 a.m., and then near the accident site at approximately 12:30 p.m. One individual reported seeing the climber off route to the north and attempted to advise the climber back toward the standard east face route. With 5.6 climbing and some rotten rock, the Black Chimney is considerably more difficult than the 4th-class east face route, making careful route-finding to stay on the standard route essential. (*Source: Ranger Ken Kreis, Grand Teton National Park.*)

FALL ON ROCK
Wind River Range, Haystack Mountain

On August 23, I (the Climber, 29) was leading the first pitch of Minor Dihedral (8 pitches, 5.9) when I got to a run-out slab section. I fell when I was 12 to 15 feet above my last cam. Due to the angle of the rock, I clipped a flake with my feet when falling, which caused my body to rotate. This led to me flip upside down, and I slammed head-first into the wall when the cam and rope arrested my fall. I broke my helmet and was knocked unconscious for approximately 30 seconds. I also suffered a deep gash in the back of my head.

After I came to, my partner lowered me to the belay, and with help from another party, got me safely back to flat ground. My partner had a Garmin inReach that we used to call for a helicopter evacuation. I suffered a concussion and a pinched nerve. All tests came back negative for skull fractures or brain damage.

The classic Minor Dihedral on the west face of Haystack Mountain. The climber in this incident fell from a run-out slab section of the 5.9 first pitch. *Steph Abegg*

ANALYSIS
I consider myself an experienced climber and have climbed long traditional routes in the alpine and on run-out terrain. My biggest lesson from this incident would be that, much like a tool needs to be sharpened, so do climbing skills. Although I was climbing something within my limits, I hadn't been trad climbing in almost four months prior to the accident. I was definitely rusty and was hopping on a route that

had heads-up terrain. If I could change things, I would have eased into this trip instead of going for a route closer to my limit on the first day. Prepare for big objectives by dialing in on smaller routes leading up to a big trip. Also, I would likely be dead if I hadn't been wearing a helmet. (*Source: The Climber.*)

OFF ROUTE RAPPEL | Improvised Rope Ascent
Devils Tower, South Face

On May 25, Climber 1 (David) and Climber 2 experienced a common rappel mishap on Devils Tower. David recounts:

I share this as a cautionary tale. After climbing the Bon Homme Variation (5.8) and then the Bailey Direct route to top out, we decided to head down by the Meadows rappels. I saw a cairn and some rap rings and rigged the rap, assuming I was on the Meadows rappel route. Boy was I wrong! After descending about 125 feet (with two 60-meter ropes), I realized I was off route. I saw a tiny ledge with a second rap anchor at 150 feet, but when I got there with no Meadows in sight, I knew I was screwed.

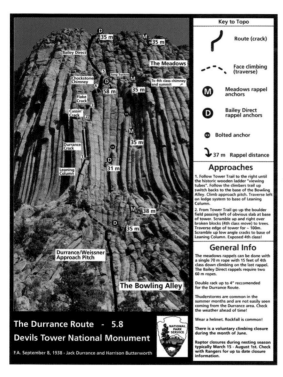

The Meadows rappel descent is surprisingly deceptive, especially given its popularity. Over a thousand people use this descent every year. *NPS Pamphlet*

There was a steady 30 mph wind with gusts to about 45. Luckily, we had a set of small radios, so I could talk with my partner. I pulled up an end and tied in and had him start belaying me. Unfortunately, the climbing was well above my grade and the rock was covered with lichen and offered no grip, so I was going nowhere fast. He started hauling me but didn't know how to rig something to assist, so I had him tie off his ATC to fix the line.

I knew the concepts of self-rescue/jugging but hadn't ever practiced. I had to quickly figure it out. I carry a Petzl Micro Traxion as well as a Sterling HollowBlock to use as a prusik. I attached the HollowBlock high and clipped into it with my rappel extension. I put the Micro Traxion low on the rope and rigged a foot stirrup with a cordelette, all while hanging in air 500 feet above the boulder field.

I figured out the method—step up on the Traxion, slide up the prusik, sit back on the prusik, pull slack through the Traxion, repeat over and over. A few times, I got to where I thought I could climb, but it was too complicated to switch from jugging to climbing.

At one point the sling to my prusik got tangled in the Traxion. Somehow I got the Traxion opened (while just hanging on the prusik) and freed the sling. It's impossible to relay the genuine fear I had during this experience. In the end it all worked out, and in about an hour I was back on top. I learned a lot.

ANALYSIS

The Meadows rappels are known to lead climbers astray and have been the location of at least one recorded fatality. The descent is unobvious, despite it being used to descend from the most popular routes on Devils Tower. With an almost 90-year rock climbing history, there are many anchors on the Tower–some at five- to ten-foot intervals–that make even well-traveled rappels problematic. As David recounts, "I should have spent more time looking around and been 100 percent sure of the descent route. The top of the Tower is disorienting if you don't pay attention to the landscape on the ground."

David was smart to carry tools for ascending a fixed rope–a little prior practice would have made his journey back to the anchor a lot easier. Learn and practice safe transitions from rappelling to ascending and the methods to back up such an ascent. Bringing radios was another good choice. David recalls, "It was very windy, and it was impossible to shout. Without the radios I'm pretty sure I would have had to call SAR. Best thirty dollars I ever spent." (Sources: David, via Mountain Project, and the Editors.)

FALL ON ROCK | Loose Rock
Guernsey State Park, Red Clove Wall

On June 30, Climber 1 (female, 27) and Climber 2 (male, 25) were climbing at the Red Clove Wall at Guernsey, a sport climbing area in far eastern Wyoming. The female climber had at least a decade of rock climbing and mountaineering experience, and had worked as a climbing guide. The male's history included five years of climbing and mountaineering, and some experience guiding. After arriving at Guernsey, the climbers consulted Mountain Project and only then learned the area was known for somewhat chossy sedimentary rock. The climbers tried to avoid holds that appeared unstable.

This accident occurred as Climber 1 belayed Climber 2 on Deep Cuts (5.8-). Five feet below the anchors, Climber 2 grabbed a ledge (reported to be 10 inches thick) that broke off. Climber 1 moved into the wall and ducked, but was struck by the falling rock between the shoulder blades.

Climber 2 clipped a personal anchor to the last bolt and verbally checked on the belayer. She was able to lower him to the base, where they assessed her injuries and called 911 after she reported pain in her spine. After evacuation, she was diagnosed with fractured T3 and T4 vertebrae.

ANALYSIS

Less frequented climbing areas often hold loose rock and other hazards. The climbers reported no sign of weakness at the collapsed ledge. Both climbers wore helmets–a wise precaution, especially in an area known for unstable rock. (Sources: Climbers 1 and 2.)

Red line shows the first two pitches of Born Again on Squamish's Apron. Instead of continuing up this route (red arrow), the climbers traversed left and climbed the second pitch of Dream On (yellow line). When their attempt to rappel (yellow arrow) failed, the leader tumbled to the ground. *Kris Wild*

CANADA

GROUND FALL | Rappel Failure
British Columbia, Squamish, The Apron

On the afternoon of September 3, Danny Dalpe (29) suffered a 200-foot ground fall from several pitches up on The Apron. At the time, Dalpe was a climber with five years of experience. Though he consistently climbed 5.13 sport routes, his multi-pitch experience was limited to two years, mainly on bolted routes around Squamish. His partner (female, 29) was a beginner climber using borrowed gear. This was her first multi-pitch outing.

Around 12:30 p.m., the pair started up Born Again, a link-up combining sections of established routes with new pitches to create "the best protected 5.10 on the Apron." Its copious protection, bolted belays, and generally forgiving angle made it a fine choice given the team's limited experience.

To avoid a party climbing above, Dalpe decided to traverse left after the second pitch. Joining Dream On (5.10b), he found the climbing changed character: The terrain was less forgiving and had only one protection bolt on the pitch. At the top of his third lead, he recalls thinking, "This was not the day I had in mind." The climbing above appeared even more demanding. "I looked up the next pitch and decided it was not worth it."

At 1:30 p.m., his climbing partner arrived at the belay, and Dalpe told her they would be descending from there. The partner carried a traditional belay/rappel device, though she was not experienced enough to rappel. Dalpe planned to use his Grigri to lower her and then make a single-line rappel, using her weight at the opposite end of the rope as a counterweight anchor. He untied his partner, threaded the rope end through the rappel rings, retied her, and then used his Grigri to lower her to a prominent ledge. Once there, she traversed to a tree anchor and connected to it with a personal anchor system (PAS). Before lowering her, Dalpe had said to his partner, "Go to the tree anchor, clip in, and do nothing."

Dalpe set up his Grigri to rappel and started down the single strand. Halfway to the tree anchor, the rope became suddenly unweighted and Dalpe tumbled down the rock. While he was falling, the rope through Dalpe's Grigri went slack and, "I saw the rope swirling orange and I kept asking, 'When am I gonna stop?'"

Dalpe hit the ground, rolled a distance, and came to rest at a tree. Climbers approaching the cliff rushed up to help. One called for an ambulance at 1:45 p.m. Another team that was on Born Again rappelled to Dalpe's partner and lowered her to the ground. At 3:45 p.m., Dalpe was transported by ambulance to the hospital.

He escaped with relatively minor injuries considering his 200-foot tumble. (He was not wearing a helmet.) He suffered a broken sternum, two broken bones in the right foot, plus multiple abrasions to his scapula and back of his head. He spent one month on a couch, and four months later he was climbing 5.13 again. (*Sources: Interview with Danny Dalpe and report from British Columbia Emergency Health Services.*)

ANALYSIS

It appears the rappel failed when Dalpe's partner somehow managed to untie her knot as he rappelled the single strand. Her half-tied figure 8 was discovered to be cinched tight. It had pulled through the rappel rings—no doubt slowing Dalpe as he tumbled toward the ground. It seems likely she began to untie as soon as she clipped into the anchor, and that some element of the system temporarily held Dalpe's weight until he had already committed to the rappel.

Counterweight systems—simul-rappelling, counter-ascending, or the descent method chosen by Dalpe in this incident—are for experts only. In fact, accidents involving such systems have claimed even very experienced climbers. The entire team needs to understand the necessity and process of maintaining a closed system until both parties are on the ground or securely anchored. Given his partner's limited experience, Dalpe could have made better choices involving the route, equipment, and rappel method.

The transition from single-pitch sport to multi-pitch routes—even on a mostly bolted climb with solid chain anchors—presents many challenges. First was equipment. This pair was equipped with a single rope and only one traditional rappel device, which necessitated a complex counterweighted rappel when they decided to bail. Another issue was experience. Dalpe's partner, through no fault of her own, was clearly in over her head.

Dalpe's physical climbing ability might have contributed indirectly to the accident. Climbing 5.13 after only a few years is an empowering—and often misleading—experience. In a multi-pitch or trad environment, a metric like a sport climbing grade is an inadequate substitute for proper tools, training, and experience. To his credit, Dalpe chose to descend when he recognized they were over their head on this long route. It takes years of practice to develop the skills and judgment to safely lead an inexperienced partner up a multi-pitch climb. (*Source: The Editors.*)

BOULDERING FALL | Missed Pads
British Columbia, East Kootenay, Bootleg Boulders

On June 16, rock season was in full swing in the East Kootenay region. The sport climbers were sending at Lakit Lake, the alpine climbers were planning for the Bugaboos, and the small community of boulderers were finding new rocks to climb.

I'm Drew Leiterman (age 31), and I've been climbing for 13 years. I had just met overstoker Steve on Facebook. He'd been scrubbing a bunch of boulders on Bootleg Mountain and was going to show me the work he'd been doing. We decided to pack only one pad each because this was mainly a recon mission with a lot of scrambling on the hillside. After a couple hours of exploring, we ended up at a nice sector about a half hour uphill from the parking area. We chucked our pads down and warmed up on some easy problems.

Hold Broke Here

Scene of the accident, with the red star marking the broken hold that caused the leg-breaking fall. The ladder was carried up earlier to help with cleaning new problems. *Drew Leiterman Collection*

We found a nice unclimbed high-ball with good holds. It started with 15 feet of incuts on vertical rock, then kicked back to a slight overhang for the last five. I climbed with ease to the top (V1-ish) only to get stumped on the final mantel. Above the lip, the rock was void of holds and was still pretty dirty. After trying unsuccessfully to figure it out, I decided to downclimb (it was well within my ability) and check it out from above.

After reversing two moves, as I moved my left hand down to another hold, my right handhold broke. I fell and somehow landed a foot away from the crash pads. Steve had been spotting me, but the combination of the height and the sudden fall made things tricky. I actually partly landed on him, throwing him back. He ended up with some pretty bad bruising on his torso.

It felt like I'd sprained my left ankle so I pulled my leg up. It was the worst-case scenario: My talus bone had exploded out the side of my foot. My foot was detached from my lower leg and held on by a bit of skin.

Like any true millennial, my first reaction was to take a selfie. Then we put on a tourniquet. We had no cell service and hadn't brought a satellite phone on our "casual" day of bouldering. We'd also scrambled up a lot of loose talus, so getting a piggyback from Steve seemed dangerous. It was close to 6:30 p.m., and we decided the best action was for Steve to run to his vehicle and get a cell signal. We'd both driven, and his car was parked below, near my van.

Almost a year prior, a friend had severed his finger and we had called SAR to get him to a hospital to get it reattached, but it took several hours for the helicopter to arrive. With that in mind and it being close to dark, I wasn't excited to wait around. I waited five minutes (which felt like hours) and started crawling down the talus to my van. For the most part it went fine, switching between scooting on my butt and downclimbing using my knees and good foot. My bad foot would flop uncontrollably and the bone would move in and out of place.

At one point I had to overcome an oven-size boulder. Just as I was getting to the bottom, the whole thing started to shift. I got out of the way, but in my haste, I touched my bloody stump on the ground. I sat there for five minutes, feeling lucky I wasn't pinned, but also looking at all the dirt I had accumulated on my wound. I was mindful that I was probably in shock and could pass out at any moment. I continued to push on. After about 45 minutes or an hour, I made it back to my van.

Steve had gone to call for help, and there was no way to communicate as I still didn't have a cell signal. My brain was in full survival mode. Nothing could stop me from getting to the hospital. I started driving. (Thankfully my van is an automatic.) I drove for 15 to 20 minutes toward town when I saw an ambulance driving toward me. I pulled over and waved them down. They were surprised, to say the least, that I was driving in my condition. Steve drove up a little after I waved down the ambulance.

In the hospital I found out that, when my foot impacted the ground, my talus bone dislocated from my calcaneus and snapped two tendons, an artery, blood vessels, nerves, and most of the ligaments on the inside of my ankle. I had two surgeries in seven days.

ANALYSIS

Fast-forward ten months and I have 80 percent mobility back. I'm climbing and working and very optimistic for a full recovery.

Thinking back, I believe Steve and I made the right decision to get me to the hospital as quickly as possible. The doctor later told me that the sooner they can operate, the better their chances for saving a foot after an accident like mine. But I don't think they would promote "hiking" or driving in that condition. I also knew that a tourniquet could cause serious complications, but I wanted to keep the blood flow to a minimum so I opted to keep it on.

I also think bouldering can be more dangerous than most people think. I fell maybe 15 feet and missed my pads by a foot or less. What would I do in the future? Bring more pads and scope the top-out before going for anything that's too tall for a fall. (*Source: Drew Leiterman.*)

RAPPEL ERROR | Uneven Ropes, No Backups
Alberta, Jasper National Park, Maligne Canyon

A party of four with two very experienced climbers and two beginners set up top-ropes on the Angel Falls ice climb in Maligne Canyon on February 17. At the top, Person 1 lowered Person 2 to the bottom of the climb (about 20 meters/65 feet), and then tied a bight in the rope and lowered Person 3 to the bottom. Person 1 then prepared to rappel but failed to readjust the ropes or tie stopper knots in the ends of the rope or any other backup. Around 2 p.m., he began to rappel and one end of the rope slipped through his brake hand and the rappel device. He fell about 15 meters (50 feet) to the canyon bottom. Efforts by medically trained first responders and eventually a paramedic failed to revive the climber.

ANALYSIS

Complacency while setting up rappels can lead to fatal errors even by the most experienced climbers. Verifying that both ends of the ropes have reached the ground—which would have been easy in this case with two climbers at the base of the route—and using backups will save your life in the long game. (*Source: Darren Vonk, Jasper Visitor Safety.*)

FALL ON ROCK | Failure to Test Hold, Protection Pulled
Alberta, Jasper National Park, Hidden Valley

Reid's broken helmet. This can happen when underestimating an "easy" route. *Jonathan Reid*

On June 27, while climbing at Hidden Valley, my partner (Person 1) and I (Jonathan Reid, 30) selected an easy trad route from the guidebook. Skipper's Rib was two pitches and rated 5.6. Both of us had climbed in this area before.

I tied in, partner-checked, and started climbing the first pitch, a 5.3 mixed gear/piton/bolt-protected lead, with Person 1 belaying. There were no obvious gear placements at first.

At eight feet, I placed a purple 0.5 Camalot in a limestone crack. It cammed well, but the crack was full of small surface crystals, and the rock appeared unstable on one side. I continued climbing five feet above the cam and pulled on a juggy hold. I fully trusted the jug without checking it, and it pulled off the wall. I took a ground fall from 12 feet up, landed on my back, and flipped over and down another three feet. The 0.5 cam had pulled out of the crack with almost no resistance.

My helmet flew off after the initial impact. I sustained back abrasions, a scalp laceration on the top/back of the head, bruises on my right arm and back, and was winded. I was able to walk to the car and required two scalp sutures in the emergency department.

ANALYSIS

My partner inspected the cam and placement right after I fell. There were obvious scars in the crack where the cam lobes had crushed the small surface crystals. The cam itself was intact. Though I recognized the placement was poor, I had not expected to fall on this easy pitch and placed the cam mostly for practice. In hindsight, there was a tree that could have been clipped three feet lower as a good first piece.

Given the established nature of the route, I also did not anticipate a hold would break so easily, and I should have tested the holds before trusting them. My helmet was very damaged and softened the impact but came off in the fall. The buckle was fine, but the chinstrap likely should have been tighter. As beginning trad climbers, both of us feel that, in the future, a bomber first piece of pro should be placed. Also, we won't underestimate a low-graded "popular" route and will test holds before trusting them. (*Source: Jonathan Reid.*)

AVALANCHE
Alberta, Columbia Icefield, Mt. Andromeda

On the morning of May 30, two Alberta climbers, Nathaniel Johnson (28) and Andrew Abel (30), were climbing the classic Skyladder on Mt. Andromeda. They were experienced climbers: Abel was an apprentice guide, and Johnson was a Level 2 climbing gym instructor.

Skyladder is the sunlit snow and ice slope on the right, leading to the top of Mt. Andromeda. *iStock.com (AutumnSkyPhotography)* [Inset] Path of the avalanche that killed two climbers on May 30. The slide traveled 900 vertical meters (3,000 feet). *Parks Canada*

Around 7:45 a.m. the climbers were caught in an avalanche. Peter Tucker, executive director of the Association of Canadian Mountain Guides, said in a press release that it cannot be determined whether the climbers were caught in the path of an avalanche that started far above them or if they somehow triggered it. He added that the slide "wasn't survivable" and that "they were carried down a slope a very long way."

Parks Canada further reported on the Mountain Information Network that the avalanche was "directly observed and reported immediately. Initial speculation is that the pair triggered the slide and were climbing, short-roped together." The report said the avalanche was a size 2.5, 60 meters (196 feet) wide, 75 centimeters (30 inches) deep, and ran for 900 meters (3,000 feet). Specific conditions data for the day were unavailable, but conditions were such that a number of other teams were climbing on Andromeda and neighboring Athabasca at the time of the avalanche.

ANALYSIS

Skyladder is a popular alpine outing that presents an attractive profile from the Trans-Canada Highway. The relatively short approach and moderate difficulty (on paper at least) make it an appealing objective. Like any mountain in a serious range like the Canadian Rockies, Andromeda requires advanced knowledge and keen avalanche awareness to climb safely. It has claimed numerous lives over the years. The "Know the Ropes" article in the 2020 edition of *Accidents* ("Avalanches: Spring and Summer Hazards for Mountaineers") is an excellent resource, available at publications.americanalpineclub. org. (*Sources: Edmonton Journal, Parks Canada, Gripped.com, and the Editors.*)

ROCKFALL

Alberta, Banff National Park, Lake Louise, Back of the Lake Crag

On May 23, several climbers were sampling some of the high-quality traditional routes at the Amphitheatre at Back of the Lake on a warm early season day. One climber was gearing up at the bottom of the cliff when a tennis ball-size rock fell from above and struck the climber in the helmet. The rock broke the helmet and knocked the person unconscious. When they regained consciousness, the climber was bleeding from their head and had pain in their neck. The climber's partners called Banff Dispatch for help.

ANALYSIS

Situational awareness is always important in identifying dangers and reducing risk, especially when it comes to overhead hazards. Though loose rock is a danger in all mountains and most cliffs, the Back of the Lake has unique hazards. Located at an elevation of about 5,740 feet, it is fairly cold much of the year and holds a deep snowpack throughout the winter and early spring. The high-quality climbing is located on a band of quartzite that is capped by a 100 to 160 feet of loose shale. Especially when the snow melts and dislodges rocks, this weaker upper shale band exposes the lower cliffs to significant falling rock or debris. In this case, it is likely the severity of the climber's injuries was reduced because they wisely wore a helmet at the base of the cliff. (*Source: Parks Canada.*)

The Amphitheatre at Back of the Lake. The solid, light-colored quartzite is topped with a tall band of dark, loose shale. *Parks Canada*

FATAL FALL | Moving Between Rappel Stations

British Columbia, Yoho National Park, Hungabee Mountain

On August 15, a party of three left their bivouac site to ascend the west ridge of Hungabee Mountain (D, 5.6). After reaching the summit, they began their descent. While in the upper third of the route, a climber rappelled, disconnected from the rope, and began to move over to the next rappel station. During this process, the climber grabbed a loose hold, which broke and resulted in the climber falling down the west face of Hungabee. The remaining two climbers immediately triggered the SOS on their satellite communication device to initiate a rescue.

A rescue team arrived by helicopter approximately 1.5 hours later. The team located the two climbers high on the ridge and spotted the deceased 32-year-old climber approximately 300 meters (984 feet) below. After surveying the scene, it was determined that the remaining two climbers would be removed from the mountain

prior to accessing the deceased. This would mini-
mize rockfall hazard from above and get the survi-
vors off the mountain before an impending storm
arrived. The two climbers were heli-slung back
down to the staging area, and the fallen climber was
then accessed and slung down to the staging area.

ANALYSIS

Transferring efficiently and safely from one rappel
to the next set of rappel anchors requires care and
an awareness of potential hazards. Whenever possible, it is best to stay tethered to the previous anchor
until you've reached the next one.

In certain cases, it's necessary to scramble from
the end of one rappel to the next station. When
practical, a quick belay may be prudent. When
scrambling unroped, it's crucial to exercise extreme
caution with loose rock. Hungabee is particularly
loose even by Canadian Rockies standards. (*Source:*
Parks Canada.)

Hungabee Mountain, with approximate line of fatal fall. *Parks Canada*

STRANDED | Insufficiently Prepared
Alberta, Banff National Park, Deltaform Mountain

On August 4, two climbers spent most of the day approaching and climbing the first
part of the Flying Buttress route (D+, 5.8) on Deltaform Mountain. This route sees
very few ascents in a regular year and, as with most of the routes in the Valley of the
Ten Peaks, is renowned for its loose rock.

The party had planned on getting a predawn start from the Moraine Lake parking
area but ended up having to wait some time for a parking spot to become available. After
starting up the approach trail and realizing one of them had forgotten a key piece of
gear, they were further delayed by having to run back to the car to retrieve that item.

Once on the route, due to the exceptionally loose rock, upward progress was
significantly slower than the climbers had anticipated. They had planned to bivouac
near the summit but by nightfall had only ascended about 300 meters (984 feet) up the
800-meter (2,600 foot) climb. The group was lucky to find a broad ledge on which to
spend the night. Overnight, the party grew more and more anxious about continuing
up the climb, and when morning broke, they used their SOS device to call for a rescue.

ANALYSIS

In the era of an exploding climbing population and social media, some climbers may
choose objectives based simply upon climbing grades or Instagram posts. These
climbers were not from the Canadian Rockies. A week prior, they had seen a social
media entry written by an experienced local alpine climber suggesting the route was
a classic and in fine shape. The climbing party put a lot of weight on this single piece
of information, which may have influenced them to underestimate the seriousness

Climbers stranded on the Flying Buttress of Deltaform Mountain. *Parks Canada*

of the route. Both were strong technical climbers with experience on solid granite cliffs but had significantly less experience dealing with the Rockies, and overestimated their ability to manage the remote and loose terrain. Choosing a less committing and better traveled route as a warmup to the area might have helped them adjust their expectations and gear list appropriately.

The party was underprepared for such a long and involved route. Although they had enough food and warm clothes for one open bivouac, they did not carry enough water to continue for multiple nights. In addition, they did not have the appropriate rope or rack for reversing the route. Other than continuing to the top, their only way off the mountain was to call for a rescue.

Helicopter rescue is complex and carries a significant amount of risk to the rescuers. In this case, it was possible for the rescue team to be inserted directly beside the climbers to sling them out. Shortly after the rescue was completed, however, the winds dramatically increased, rendering helicopter use impossible. All climbers should be prepared and capable of descent and self-rescue. Only look to external rescue as a last resort if an accident occurs or there are no other options. (*Source: Parks Canada.*)

OFF ROUTE, STRANDED |
Underestimated Route
Alberta, Banff National Park, Mt. Rundle

On October 2, a climber soloing the Rundle Traverse from Canmore to Banff requested a rescue after attempting to retreat near the end of the route. The Rundle Traverse is a long, exposed technical ridge consisting of 11 distinct peaks. The ridge has significant route-finding challenges, with several unmarked rappels and a technical grade of about 5.5.

On a clear, sunny day, after traveling a significant portion of the ridge, the solo climber reached the section before the 11th peak. Unable to find the best route through the exposed terrain, the climber attempted to retreat down the southwest slope of the mountain to the valley. While retreating, the climber encountered several cliff bands they were unable to navigate. Eventually, the combination of exposed terrain, fatigue, and incoming darkness led the climber to call for help. In the final minutes of daylight, the local rescue team was able to locate and extract the unharmed climber via helicopter long-line.

ANALYSIS

Despite the low technical grade, the Rundle Traverse, like many undertakings in the Canadian Rockies, is a serious objective and not to be underestimated. For much of its 12-mile length, the ridge involves poor rock quality and exposed, complex terrain. The average time to complete the route is between 11 and 16 hours. By October in the Canadian Rockies, the sun sets around 7 p.m. These shorter days provide less daylight to complete an objective of this length, and the limited daylight also plays a factor in the ability to carry out a rescue.

Along the ridge are many opportunities to retreat down the southwest slopes of Rundle. However, there are many places that appear suitable to descend, yet retreat actually is not possible. Preplanning exit spots along the ridge helps to ensure a successful escape if needed.

The climber selected a good weather window, and the route was in good condition, free of snow and ice. They were carrying an appropriate communication device and were able to call for help, which allowed for a successful rescue. (*Source: Parks Canada.*)

FALL ON ROCK | Broken Hold, Protection Pulled
Alberta, Kananaskis Country, East End of Mt. Rundle

On July 10, a party of two was climbing Generosity (13 pitches, 5.9), a long, mixed-protection route near Canmore. On pitch seven, the leader pulled off a loose rock, which caused him to fall 30 to 40 feet. A piece of gear pulled out early in the fall. The climber fell down terrain that was less than vertical, hitting multiple ledges. He severely injured his hand, but fortunately nothing else. Both climbers were well equipped, wearing helmets, and they were climbing within their technical limit.

A nearby climbing party assisted the pair, and an evacuation was performed by helicopter, using several long-line operations to access the cliff face.

ANALYSIS

Testing holds and having more experience with loose rock would have helped but would not have eliminated the risk. On longer routes in the Rockies, the rock is notoriously loose and unpredictable. Even popular routes like Generosity are not climbed enough to be choss-free.

Managing loose rock requires a climbing technique involving balance with multiple contact points versus a more committed sport climbing style of movement. For example, having both hands pulling on the same hold can be problematic if the hold breaks. Also, the reliability of cams and nuts depends on rock integrity. In this case, a piece of gear failed, adding to the length of the fall. (*Source: Kananaskis Public Safety.*)

Silver Basin on the day of a slide that caught six skiers and killed one of them. The avalanche broke widely near the rim of the basin and ran 650 vertical feet. *Northwest Avalanche Center*

BACKCOUNTRY AVALANCHES

This section examines a selection of U.S. avalanche accidents involving backcountry skiers and snowboarders during the most recent winter season, December 2021 through March 2022. They were selected to cover a variety of accidents and geographic locations. The narratives and analyses have been adapted from reports published by regional avalanche centers.

LARGE GROUP CAUGHT IN SLIDE

Washington, Silver Basin (Crystal Mountain)

On the morning of Saturday, December 11, the first major winter storm of the season was impacting the Cascades. Until this point, thin snow cover had limited backcountry recreation opportunities. A group of six ski tourers decided to travel in the Silver Basin area of Crystal Mountain ski resort due to its generally good early season coverage and easy access. Weather stations at the ski area recorded 11 inches of new snow on Friday night, with an additional five inches falling on Saturday. Wind speeds averaged 40–50 mph, with a gust up to 90 mph recorded during the storm. The Silver Basin area of the resort was not yet open, and ski patrol had not conducted any avalanche mitigation work for the season. As a result, the basin contained a "backcountry" snowpack.

The group left the parking lot and ascended the approved uphill travel route through a section of the open ski resort. As they neared Silver Basin, the group broke trail, staying within the ski area boundary. Members of the team noted the stormy weather, including continued snowfall and blowing snow. While the group may have noticed these possible signs of unstable snow, they did not discuss them during a short break near the bottom of the basin. Instead, they decided to continue ascending toward a prominent low point in the ridgeline called Silver Saddle.

The party traveled close together as they continued to break trail across a long ascending traverse. About 250 feet shy of the saddle, members of the team reported seeing cracking and felt "the snow change." They immediately switchbacked, hoping to find a location near some rocks to transition for the ski down. It was at this moment that the slope released. All members of the group were immediately caught in the moving torrent of snow. The avalanche failed about 200 feet above their heads, was nearly 600 feet wide, and ran 650 vertical feet.

Three members of the team were carried 250 feet downhill and deposited close together. Skiers 1 and 3 were only partially buried and able to quickly free themselves. Skier 3 immediately called 911 and was patched through to Crystal Mountain ski patrol. Skier 2 was located, fully buried, and was found not breathing but with a pulse. After the other skiers cleared his airway and rolled Skier 2 on his side, he began to breathe.

The other three members of the team were carried further down the slope, past a small treed knoll, and deposited in a scattered group. Even though he traveled to near the toe of the debris, Skier 6 was mostly on the surface and was able to begin searching for his teammates. He rapidly located and uncovered Skier 5. A nearby party that witnessed the event also responded. Witness 1 quickly located Skier 4 with his beacon and probe. Skier 4 had been carried through a stand of small trees, over a short cliff, and was buried under about a foot of debris. Witness 1 immediately noticed obvious signs of trauma. After clearing the airway, he began performing CPR. Unfortunately, Skier 4 did not respond to any of these interventions. Eventually all members of the party decided to retreat to a safer location due to the ongoing storm. Ski patrol and other rescuers responded to the scene and assisted the remainder of party back to the trailhead.

ANALYSIS

Accidents like this provide several learning outcomes. Much of this information was collected through post-accident interviews between involved parties and the Northwest Avalanche Center. We appreciate these individuals sharing their story so others can learn from this tragedy.

While all members of the party reportedly checked the avalanche forecast for Saturday, the selection of Silver Basin was based on coverage and early season ski quality instead of potential avalanche conditions. This factor may have been compounded by lack of familiarity with the terrain. Many members of the team had been to the area, but only once or twice. Only one individual had significant experience traveling in Silver Basin. This resulted in that person becoming the de facto leader. While not their intent, having only one member of the group familiar with the terrain significantly changed the team's decision-making process. As mentioned above, several individuals noticed the ongoing storm and possible signs of unstable snow, but they continued onward despite these concerns.

SEASON SUMMARY

The 2021–2022 season was well below average for avalanche fatalities in the United States, with 17 fatalities, compared with an average of 27 deaths during the previous 10 winter seasons. Six of the victims were skiers or snowboarders, six were snowmobilers, four were climbers, hikers, or snowshoers, and one was riding a motorized snow bike.

While ascending toward the saddle, and well within the start zone of the avalanche path, the group was traveling very close together. This travel technique may have better enabled communication among the large team, especially in the stormy weather, but it also exposed all members to the hazard simultaneously. As a result, all six teammates were caught and carried in the avalanche. It is only by a matter of luck that at least some of the group remained on the surface, uninjured and able to assist in the rescue.

One bright spot in these events was the quick and effective rescue of two fully buried teammates. This emphasizes the potential for well-practiced and executed avalanche rescue to save lives. The team and responding witnesses should be commended for these quick actions. It also highlights the impact of terrain traps on fatal outcomes. While all members of the group were caught and carried, the sole fatality was a result of traumatic injuries inflicted by traveling through trees and over rocks. (*Source: Northwest Avalanche Center.*)

PERSISTENT WEAK LAYER | Various Human Factors
Wyoming, Teton Range, Game Creek

A party of eight had been staying at the Plummer Canyon Yurt for several days. On March 17, 2022, five of the members skied a couple of low-angle runs and some trees on nearby Mt. Wow (10,262 feet), with no signs of instability except for one collapse or whumpf on low-angle terrain.

In midafternoon, one of the more experienced group members led the party toward a north-facing slope (Danford's Bowl) dropping toward Game Creek. The intent was to ski in pitches to reach a bench above a terrain funnel and then exit skier's left to skin back toward the yurt. The first skier planned to descend near trees on the skier's right side of the bowl, and warned the others to stay to the right of two tracks laid by skiers one hour earlier. He skied the pitch to a safe zone near the trees, and the rest of the party skied the pitch one at at time and gathered below dense trees.

Skier 1 left the safe zone first. He stopped just above the team's planned exit on skier's left and directly in the avalanche path. Skier 2 continued past Skier 1 and onto the bench. Skier 3 then stopped near Skier 1 and sat down in the snow. Finally, Skier 4 dropped in and rode close to the left boundary made by the previous pair of tracks. As he skied by the leader of the first pitch, still watching from the trees, the slope released. Skier 4 turned safely out of the path, but Skiers 1 and 3 were carried downslope into the narrow confines of the exit gully and out into the fan of debris, for a total vertical distance of 525 feet.

After identifying the point where the two skiers were last seen, the remaining skiers switched their avalanche beacons to search and side-slipped into the tight gully below. As they neared the fanned-out debris, they noticed a hand or article of clothing in the snow. As Skier 4 continued following the other beacon signal, the remaining skiers began to dig out the buried victim. They soon reached Skier 3's face, which had a bluish tinge from early cyanosis. After receiving rescue breaths, the buried Skier 3 regained respiratory drive.

Meanwhile, a little higher in the debris, Skier 4 pinpointed Skier 1, who was detected 0.8 meters beneath the surface, and began to dig. Shortly afterward, two local skiers who had witnessed the avalanche arrived on the scene and began to help. After approximately 15 minutes of digging, the rescuers began CPR on Skier 1 (age 61) and continued for 30 minutes without success.

ANALYSIS

During an interview following the incident, one of the more experienced members of the group related that the team had seen "a whole lot of green" in the avalanche forecast in the days leading up to the accident. While this is true, these Low danger ratings were for the middle and lower elevation bands of the forecast area, while the upper elevation band—starting just 200 vertical feet above the slide's start zone at 8,800 feet—had the higher hazard rating of Moderate.

This hard slab avalanche occurred on a north-northeast-facing slope with an average angle at the crown of about 42°. The slab slid on a 1cm layer of faceted snow over a hard melt-freeze crust, a layer likely formed after a widespread avalanche cycle in early January. Local guides who had skied this same slope and professional avalanche workers all were surprised when this layer reactivated in the Tetons forecast zone, where the snowpack generally was deep. However, the snow where this avalanche occurred was much shallower than would be expected in the Tetons. Several other human-triggered avalanches occurred during this period in areas with a relatively thin snowpack or on the old bed surface of prior avalanches.

Five skiers dropped in to this north-facing slope one at a time near point A, planning to exit to skier's left (arrow). The group's second pitch began where Skier 5 waited and watched. Skiers 1 and 3 stopped in the middle of the slide path, while Skier 2 continued to the bench to skier's left. Skier 4's run then triggered an avalanche that swept Skiers 1 and 3 down the gully. The skier buried at point B died in the incident, while the skier at point C was saved. *Bridger-Teton Avalanche Center*

It's important to recognize that elevation bands and forecast zones exist as aids to understanding where the danger may be found, not as an absolute guide to the extent of the danger. Referring to information in adjacent forecast zones and elevation bands can shed light on potential avalanche problems and aid in route planning and decision-making.

This accident seems particularly tragic since more disciplined safe-travel techniques likely would have led to a different outcome. This group skied one at a time on this line and at first used an island of safety at the edge of the path as they descended. The first skier instructed the team to avoid the steep and potentially wind-loaded left side of the gully. Despite these efforts at careful route-planning at the beginning of the run, the deceased Skier 1 stopped in the middle of the avalanche path and Skier

3 chose to stop next to Skier 1. Perhaps fatigue led to these decisions or they were simply a reaction to negative feedback gained from seeing no recent avalanche activity and only one clear sign of unstable snow (the collapse heard earlier in the day). Many human factors may be at play with a large group, which is more challenging to manage effectively in such constricted and consequential terrain. A discussion on human factors and group dynamics is always worthwhile when entering avalanche terrain, especially with a large group. (*Source: Bridger-Teton Avalanche Center.*)

VERY LONG BURIAL AND RESCUE
Utah, Wasatch Range, Silver Fork

On March 12, 2022, a party of six, with two guides, ascended from Grizzly Gulch in Little Cottonwood Canyon toward East Bowl Pass overlooking Silver Fork, which flows north into Big Cottonwood Canyon. While traveling, the group separated into Group A and Group B, planning to ski different routes and then regroup below Silver Fork's West Bowl. Group A consisted of four clients and one guide, moving at a bit faster pace, while Group B consisted of two clients and one guide.

After climbing to the rim of East Bowl, Group A ascended to East Peak, safely descended the northwest ridge and East Bowl, and then waited for Group B on a bench above a gully at the base of West Bowl. Group B arrived at East Bowl Pass and headed up Davenport Hill to ski Cabin Ridgeline northward into Silver Fork, where they would meet the skiers of Group A.

Group B descended Cabin Ridgeline one at a time in pitches. On the final ski pitch to join Group A, the first skier safely descended. While the second skier was midway down the pitch, an avalanche released above them. The party below yelled "Avalanche!" and the skier was able to head off the slope and away from the slide. However, the guide at the top of the pitch was caught, carried, and fully buried down in the gully below.

At approximately 12:30 p.m., one of the party members called 911 and the group quickly booted toward the debris pile. After a beacon search and positive probe strike deep under the surface, the skiers dug furiously, extracted the patient, and cleared his airway. It took 23 minutes from the time the avalanche was initially triggered to the time the skier's airway was cleared.

The skier was breathing and had a pulse when the airway was cleared. Having been strained through trees in the avalanche, he experienced trauma on his face and torso [six broken ribs, a bruised lung, and facial lacerations, according to a published report].

Five minutes after the buried skier was recovered, Solitude ski patrol arrived on the scene. The skier was hoisted out by Lifeflight around 2:30 p.m.; he was in critical but stable condition. The remaining party members skied out with Solitude ski patrol.

ANALYSIS
The Utah Avalanche Center had issued a Special Avalanche Bulletin for the day of the accident. The forecast avalanche hazard was Considerable on north to east aspects at all elevations, following a week of stormy weather that buried a weak layer of faceted snow formed during a period of drought in January and February. Clearing skies and a sunny weekend lured many skiers out despite the hazard. The avalanche center's bulletin for March 12 warned, "Dangerous avalanche conditions combined

with great powder and beautiful weather make accidents likely. There have been many close calls this week, but luck eventually runs out."

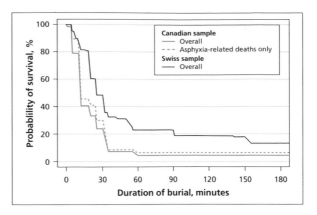

A 2011 study examined survival of people completely buried in avalanches in Canada and Switzerland between 1980 and 2005. In both cases the survival rate plunged after 15 to 20 minutes of burial, but the survival rate fell quicker in Canada. A maritime snow climate, with wetter and denser snow, was associated with the fastest drops in survival rate. *Haegeli-Falk-Brugger-Etter-Boyd*

The guides in this party were Winslow Passey, who led Group A, and Willie Benegas, who led Group B and was buried and rescued in the avalanche. Passey is an AMGA-certified ski mountaineering guide with over two decades of experience, and Benegas is among the most experienced high-elevation guides working in North America. In a personal account of the accident included with the Utah Avalanche Center report, Passey reported that the whole party had discussed the avalanche hazard and performed beacon checks before the tour, and during the initial ascent they dug three pits to assess conditions. Passey also said she carefully checked slope angles all day using a shaded Cal Topo map, in order to stay away from steeper terrain.

In an interview in *Outside*, Benegas attributed the accident to overconfidence, estimating he had skied this same slope 150 times without incident. "It has been an extremely difficult year," Benegas told *Outside*. "Our snowpack has been challenging to forecast on the micro-terrain assessment aspect."

The Utah Avalanche Center report said a couple of things went right for [Benegas] that could have very easily gone wrong:

- *The skier lived despite being buried for 23 minutes under nearly two meters of snow.* [The first probe strike was at 1.5 meters, but Benegas was facing diagonally downhill; the rescuers first uncovered his boot and pack and had to dig extensively to reach his face and clear his airway.] Below the 15-minute mark in a burial, the probability of survival drops rapidly. At the 23-minute mark, the probability drops to 35 percent.
- *A skilled team was close by.* Since [Benegas] was the last in his group at the top of the pitch, and Group A was already at the bottom of the slope, in most situations like this the rescuers would have had to transition back to uphill ski mode to reach the burial site. In this case, they were able to reach the site on foot, saving them valuable time. As well, the two clients with Group B had less avalanche training than the members of Group A. The close location of Group A allowed the more experienced members to run the rescue.
- This easily could have been a multi-burial situation. At the time of the avalanche, two skiers were within the path. (*Sources: Utah Avalanche Center, Outside.com.*)

MID-TOUR CHANGE OF PLANS

Colorado, Sawatch Range, Mt. Peck

On March 10, 2022, two backcountry riders set out for an outing near Mt. Peck (12,208 feet), about 1.5 miles southeast of Monarch Pass. Rider 1 traveled on skis and Rider 2 on a snowboard. They brought their dog along for the tour. The plan was to ascend the northwest ridge of Mt. Peck to near the summit and possibly descend lower-angle terrain along the northeast ridge into the North Fooses Creek drainage.

During their ascent, they decided instead to descend a steep northeast-facing slope before reaching the summit. Rider 1 skied a short distance down in forested terrain on the skier's right side of the slope. Rider 2 then descended a short distance past Rider 1, still staying in the trees. They commented on the lack of a slab and no cracking or collapsing, and decided to finish their descent further skier's left, down steeper and more open terrain. They identified a point to meet in low-angle terrain about 500 feet downslope from the steeper headwall. Rider 2 descended first and stopped at the regroup point without incident. Rider 1 then sent the dog down, who reached Rider 2 safely.

As Rider 1 began his descent, he triggered an avalanche on his second turn. He was immediately swept off his feet and deployed his airbag. He was carried around 400 vertical feet before ending up against a tree, lying on his side with avalanche debris covering his face. He was able to free an arm and clear his face after "an eternity of seconds." He had lost one ski.

Rider 2 described the collapse of the slope as severe enough to knock her over while standing with her feet strapped into her snowboard. She could see the avalanche coming, but did not have time to deploy her airbag. The avalanche washed over her and the dog, carrying her down the slope. When the avalanche stopped, she was face down and covered by less than a foot of snow. A portion of her helmet and snowboard were visible on the surface. She had been buried with one hand very close to her face, and she was able to pull off her glove with her teeth and move her fingers enough to clear snow from her face. She started yelling for Rider 1, who quickly located and extricated her.

The riders began looking for their dog, but there were no visible clues or tracks in the area. They probed the debris for approximately an hour, but did not locate the dog. They made the difficult decision to leave the scene and head back to the trailhead, strapping a shovel to Rider 1's foot so he could make his way out with just one ski.

Two days after the accident, motorists came upon the dog near the top of Monarch Pass. He was reunited with the owners.

ANALYSIS

The avalanche occurred on a very steep (40°) north-facing slope near treeline. It was a hard slab avalanche, medium-size relative to the path. The avalanche broke three to five feet deep on a layer of faceted crystals that were first buried by a storm on February 21. As the avalanche ran, it gouged down into snow layers near the ground in the steepest and rockiest areas of the path.

The Colorado Avalanche Information Center's (CAIC) forecast for the Sawatch zone on the day of the avalanche was Considerable (Level 3) danger near and above

DOGS IN AVALANCHE TERRAIN

During the 2021-22 season, in Colorado alone, three dogs were killed in avalanche incidents along with human companions. In other cases, dogs—and their owners—narrowly escaped avalanches. In one incident at the popular Berthoud Pass riding zone, on December 26, 2021, a dog triggered an avalanche that swept it about 300 yards to the bottom of a chute and buried the animal. The owner and witnesses initially used their transceivers to search for potentially buried people, and then, finding nothing, they probed for 15 to 20 minutes until, happily, one of them found the dog alive and unharmed.

Apollo triggered an avalanche above Berthoud Pass, Colorado, and was buried but recovered. *Colorado Avalanche Information Center*

Many dogs love snow, and winter travel with a pet can be a joyful experience. But dogs that aren't trained for avalanche duty can easily run into a hazardous area, and animal companions add complexity to decision-making and a significant element of uncertainty in avalanche terrain. (The slide triggered by the dog at Berthoud Pass had the potential to bury any skier below, and the search for the buried pooch exposed several people to additional risk.) If you choose to travel in avalanche terrain with a dog, the animal should be highly responsive to voice commands. Terrain choices should be more conservative than usual. And dogs should never be outfitted with an avalanche beacon. We love our pets, but a signal from a pet's beacon could cause a life-threatening delay to the search for possible buried people. —*The Editors*

treeline and Moderate (Level 2) below treeline. After a series of storms in the preceding couple of weeks, accompanied by moderate to strong winds, slab avalanches were listed as the first problem in the forecast.

The pair of riders was aware of dangerous avalanche conditions and read the avalanche forecast the morning of the accident. They had toured in the Monarch Pass area several days earlier and dug a snow profile on a similar aspect and elevation to the slope that avalanched. They did not observe any obvious signs of instability traveling along the ridge nor on their descent of the upper slope. They committed to a very steep slope based in part on these limited observations—obvious signs of instability are not always present before you trigger an avalanche.

An important factor is that they deviated from their original plan by choosing a steeper descent while on their tour. Numerous accidents can be attributed to groups changing their plans on the fly and traveling into terrain they had previously ruled out as too dangerous.

The pair chose their regroup location based on observations of avalanches on the slope in previous years. However, this avalanche broke deeper and wider than they anticipated, and the debris ran over Rider 2 at the regroup point. Avalanches failing on persistent weak layers can break in surprising ways, and it is critical to give steep terrain wide buffers to address this uncertainty.

We do not know if the dog was buried and dug himself out of the avalanche debris or if he was spooked by the event and ran from the scene. It is a surprising and happy outcome that the dog made his way back to the trailhead and eventually was reunited with the pair. Only the dog will ever know the full story of what happened. (*Source: Colorado Avalanche Information Center.*)

DEEPLY BURIED WEAK LAYER | Familiarity Heuristic
Colorado, Park Range, North Fork of Fish Creek

On March 19, 2022, two backcountry skiers planned a trip to an area locally known as the Dome in the North Fork of Fish Creek, about eight miles east of the town of Steamboat Springs. Skier 1 arrived at the Dry Lake trailhead around 8:30 a.m. While he waited for Skier 2, he read the Colorado Avalanche Information Center (CAIC) forecast and noted that it listed a persistent slab avalanche problem in all elevation bands on northwest, north, northeast, and east-facing aspects. He then made a quick ski run on a low-angle, west-facing slope near the parking lot. He felt the snow was stable in this area.

When Skier 2 arrived, the two unloaded snowmobiles and rode east up County Road 38 for about 11 miles to Buffalo Pass, then continued toward the Dome and parked their snowmobiles. Skier 2 had been in the area many times and took the lead as they skinned across three small knobs to reach the spot where Skier 2 planned to descend into the North Fork of Fish Creek.

Starting first, Skier 2 descended 100 to 200 vertical feet on a treed slope and waited for Skier 1. They did not see any cracking in the snow or hear any whumpfing. The two traversed eastward until they were above a steeper, sparsely treed part of the slope. During the traverse, Skier 1 pushed with his downhill ski to see if he "could get snow to move." He saw no indications of unstable snow.

Skier 2 headed down into the steeper, more open area while Skier 1 waited. After Skier 2 made one turn, the whole slope dropped, making a large whumpf. Cracks shot out around Skier 2 as the avalanche broke two to three feet above him. The moving snow swept him down the hill and out of sight.

Skier 1 turned his transceiver to receive before the avalanche came to a stop. He could see rocks in the spot where Skier 2 triggered the slide, and he picked his way down through them and over a rollover until he could see Skier 2 pinned against a tree with his back facing uphill. Snow had piled up behind him, and he was not moving.

After clearing snow out of Skier 2's mouth, Skier 1 gave him rescue breaths, but the patient did not respond. Skier 1 called 911, cleared the avalanche debris from Skier 2's back to create a flat spot, and began CPR, which he continued for about an hour without success. Routt County Search and Rescue and Classic Air Medical responded, and Skier 1 was evacuated by air. Skier 2's body was recovered the following day.

ANALYSIS

This was a soft slab avalanche, small relative to the size of the path, that released on a 40° northwest-facing slope. The avalanche broke on a persistent weak layer of faceted crystals buried 18 to 28 inches deep, in the middle of the snowpack. Snow layers this weak are not common in the Park Range, and it is especially unusual to see a layer this weak—this deep in the snowpack—and still reactive in mid-March. However, the danger posed by this layer was well documented in the avalanche forecasts and reports of avalanche activity in the Steamboat and Flat

Aerial image of avalanche start zone in the North Fork of Fish Creek, Colorado. Arrow indicates the track of Skier 2. The circle is where Skier 2 likely triggered the avalanche. *Colorado Avalanche Information Center*

Tops zone; one week earlier, a snowmobiler triggered an avalanche that broke on the same weak layer, 40 miles to the north, with fatal consequences.

Skier 2 had many years of experience in the Park Range and skied in and around the Fish Creek drainage with some regularity. We will never know his decision-making process on the day of the accident. However, people's tendency to rely on familiar places and situations to help them make decisions is well documented (Herbert, 2010). When we are accustomed to behaving in a certain way in a certain area, it can be very difficult to recognize unusual conditions and change our approach.

Modern avalanche safety courses teach a trip-planning process that includes using the avalanche forecast to determine the type of terrain you want to avoid, then reviewing your route to ensure it keeps you away from the dangerous areas. On the day of the accident, the two skiers did not discuss the avalanche forecast or the details of their plan before departing the trailhead. Skier 1 knew the forecast warned of persistent slab avalanches on northerly slopes; however, although he knew the general destination for the day, he did not know the terrain well enough to match it with the information in the forecast and decide in advance if their route was appropriate.

Persistent slab avalanches are difficult to predict and are especially dangerous when they do not provide the feedback we expect, like cracking and collapsing in the snow. The best strategy during these periods is to use the avalanche forecast to identify terrain features where this type of avalanche is possible and avoid them. (*Source: Colorado Avalanche Information Center.*)

TRIGGERED AVALANCHE CATCHES TWO PARTIES
New Hampshire, Mt. Washington, Tuckerman Ravine

On December 5, 2021, winds were light in Tuckerman Ravine and temperatures seasonally cold, with poor visibility near the top of the ravine. During the five days prior, one to three inches of new snow was recorded on Mt. Washington's summit each day, with varying wind from the west and northwest.

Several parties were climbing or skiing in the ravine on December 5. In late morning, two skiers climbed to the top of Left Gully, evaluating the snowpack along the way using hand-shear tests. They found softer snow than expected but no obvious signs of instability. Near the top, where the gully opens up, they noted a shallow pillow of wind-drifted snow (maximum of six inches deep) to the right, and they moved up left to avoid the hazard. They transitioned to skis at the top with poor visibility. Both were prepared with avalanche beacons, shovels, and probes.

Below them, a solo skier reached his high point, approximately halfway up the gully, and began to transition for skiing, unaware of the two skiers above. His avalanche beacon had been turned on well before he entered avalanche terrain.

The two skiers above made a plan to ski the steeper entry on the right, appropriately skiing one at a time. When the first skier descended, a soft slab released, pulling the skier off his feet. He was swept down with the debris, and when he and debris reached the constricted portion of the gully, a larger, deeper avalanche was triggered, with a crown line that ran wall to wall, approximately 20 to 26 inches at the highest point. This skier was carried approximately 800 vertical feet by the avalanche, coming to a stop at the entrance of the gully. He was unhurt and on top of the snow.

The solo skier had not yet removed his crampons when he was caught by the same avalanche and carried approximately 450 vertical feet, encountering rocks along the way and arriving at a point further downhill than the first skier. He was on top of the snow with serious injuries requiring immediate medical attention.

The remaining skier descended on skis with continued poor visibility, looking for clues to help find potential victims. He quickly found his partner (the first skier) and the injured solo skier. A beacon search of the debris was conducted to rule out additional buried victims. The two uninjured skiers aided the solo skier until additional help arrived. The patient was packaged in a rescue litter, and a team consisting of USFS snow rangers, the Harvard Cabin caretaker, the two uninjured skiers, and several kind bystanders spent the next four hours carrying and dragging the patient litter to an ambulance waiting at the trailhead, arriving at approximately 5:30 p.m.

ANALYSIS

Anytime there is new snow and wind, you are likely to find slabs of drifted snow with the potential to avalanche when an additional load such as a skier or climber is added. This can and does occur before the Mount Washington Avalanche Center begins issuing a daily avalanche forecast with a hazard rating.

In early season, when terrain options for skiing are limited, certain features may concentrate skiers. Left Gully had been a very popular destination over the previous few weeks, with snow coverage top to bottom. This gully is long, with no options to escape until the bottom opens up. With poor visibility, it may be impossible to see if anyone is above or below, adding an additional hazard. Early season excitement, limited terrain to ski, a shallow snowpack with rock-filled runouts, poor visibility, and recent wind-drifted snow are all factors that contributed to this unfortunate event.

It's worth remembering that winter is long with (hopefully) plenty of snow to ski. Slow down, think carefully about decisions you make, and consider that your actions may also impact others. (*Source: Mount Washington Avalanche Center.*)

Clear skies finally allow a helicopter to approach the summit of Mt. Sneffels in Colorado after a severe storm trapped an injured man and prompted an all-night rescue. *OMRT Photo*

SEARCH AND RESCUE AWARDS

Rocky Talkie and the AAC partnered in early 2022 to solicit nominations for the Rocky Talkie Search and Rescue Awards. These awards recognize stand-out rescues from the previous year; $25,000 in grant funding is split among the winning teams. (Rocky Talkie allocates $2 from every radio sold to SAR funding.) More than 5,000 people voted on the top nominations, and the lead vote-getter and three runners-up are highlighted below. For detailed stories and photos, visit rockytalkie.com/SARaward.

OURAY MOUNTAIN RESCUE
July 30, 2021

As the worst storm of the summer bore down on tiny Ouray, Colorado, a handful of climbers hustled to descend nearby Mt. Sneffels (14,157 feet). Sneffels' summit is guarded by several moves of tricky climbing, now coated with verglas. One of the climbers, a 50-year-old man, slipped and cartwheeled past his hiking partner, falling 40 feet to rocks below.

The partner scrambled down to check on him and immediately called for a rescue. In early afternoon, dispatchers contacted Ouray Mountain Rescue Team (OMRT). "Confirmed fatality," the message read. "Send help." Just 25 minutes later, the team got a second message: "Cancel." Not sure what to expect, the volunteers loaded gear into rescue vehicles and made a beeline for the remote trailhead.

By the time they arrived, the fallen climber's partner and a few other hikers had made it down to the base of the mountain. The storm had hit the peak while they waited for help, and between flashing lighting, sheeting rain, and sub-20°F temperatures, it hadn't been safe for them to stay with the injured man. They said the man was alive, but badly injured. OMRT volunteers made sure the victim's partner got proper care and then waited in their vechicles for a break in the weather. By now the man had been lying in the rocks, drenched and freezing, for at least six hours. The odds for survival weren't looking good.

The storm cell eventually sputtered out, and Grant Kleeves, a longtime OMRT volunteer and accomplished mountaineer, OMRT lieutenant Patrick Brighton, and two other rescuers started hiking up the mountain. As the rescuers approached the narrow bench where the patient lay, Kleeves called out to the man and saw his eyelids flicker. Shocked, Kleeves turned around: "Get on the radio—he's still alive!"

The patient had entered the late stages of hypothermia. When that happens, the body sends out a final burst of heat. Though he was literally dying from cold, the patient had shrugged out of his jacket and started to remove his shirt. It's a phenomenon called "paradoxical undressing."

The rescuers started assessing the patient, wrapped him in sleeping bags, and gave him oxygen. They soon found he'd fractured his skull—and that there was no way he could be safely carried down the mountain without doing further damage.Brighton, a surgeon in his day job, listened to the man's erratic breathing. He radioed down to base camp: "We don't think he's going to survive the night."

OMRT captain Ruth Stewart had made multiple calls to request helicopter support, but the operators said flying in these conditions wouldn't be possible. By now it was pitch black and there was more bad weather coming. Brighton's team would have to stay put. So, the four volunteers on the mountain unpacked their one remaining sleeping bag and huddled against the rock. It was going to be a long night.

As the patient's muscles began to warm up and he became more alert, he grew combative. He started rolling, clawing at his oxygen, and trying to walk off the narrow platform. The rescuers tried to calm the man, but nothing worked. Dodging flailing limbs, they held him down. Ultimately, they had to clip him to an anchor they'd built, effectively tying him to the mountain.

For the first four hours of the night, the rescuers took turns sitting with their legs draped over the patient, both to keep him warm and to keep him from throwing himself off the ledge. Around midnight, the patient fell into a deeper sleep. His condition seemed to be stabilizing, but the rescuers were still worried. They were in radio contact with doctors at the local hospital, but there was only so much they could do. The only option was to keep the patient warm and wait.

Meanwhile, far below the summit, the rain and hail had swelled into a landslide that took out the narrow mountain road to the trailhead. Brighton's team was cut off. Then a local miner named Bumper Williams called the team. Ouray is a small town, and Williams had heard about the ongoing rescue. He volunteered to bring a bulldozer from the mine and clear the road. Within minutes, the operation was back on track.

Up on the mountain, with his medications and oxygen resupplied, the patient's breathing started to even out. The rescuers switched out heat packs regularly, working through exhaustion to keep him warm. Around 4 a.m., as a hint of light peered above the horizon, Kleeves heard mumbling. He turned.

"Why are you sitting on me?!" the patient asked.

Kleeves couldn't help but smile. Looking down at the man they'd fought to save—and fought with—all night, he felt a wave of gratitude. A few hours later, just as the sun peeked over the saddle, the patient was airlifted off the peak.

TAHOE NORDIC SEARCH AND RESCUE
January 28, 2021

Ten feet of snow over three days had loaded every chute west of Lake Tahoe virtually to the breaking point. On his last run of the day, a snowboarder took a wrong turn at Sugar Bowl Resort and carved down into a ravine called Coldstream Canyon. By the time he realized he was lost, retracing his steps was impossible in the chest-deep snow. The snowboarder, an off-duty California Highway Patrol officer in his mid-40s, used his phone to call for help as darkness fell.

Even though the man was only a mile away, ski patrol believed there was no safe way to reach him from above, given the extreme avalanche danger. Poring over a map, the Tahoe Nordic SAR team laid two plans: One group would attempt to ski a circuitous five-mile route over lower-angle terrain, while another would head directly up the canyon with a Sno-cat and three snowmobiles. When the Cat bogged down, 1.5 miles from the snowboarder, rescuers fought through the deep snow on foot. It took another three hours to reach the patient, just before 1 a.m., where they outfitted him with snowshoes and started for home.

LARIMER COUNTY SEARCH AND RESCUE
July 19, 2021

The Happy Hour Crag in northern Colorado's Poudre Canyon is named because it's quite close to the road and easy to access after work. But when a climber at the crag fell 30 feet and suffered an open fracture in his back, the ensuing rescue in complex terrain made a mockery of the Happy Hour name.

To access the patient, a man in his early 20s, Larimer County SAR teams had to be ferried across the Cache La Poudre River, climb a loose 250-foot gully, and traverse a narrow ledge across the multi-tiered cliff. As medics treated the climber and packaged him in a litter, one of the team members rappelled off the ledge to scope a descent route through a narrow chimney. They started down with the patient around 1 a.m. After lowering him down the cliff and scree gully, he was ferried across the river and then hauled up a steep bank to the road, arriving shortly before dawn.

LAS VEGAS METROPOLITAN POLICE SEARCH AND RESCUE
October 20, 2021

Nearing the top of the Red Rock Canyon classic Epinephrine, two brothers were simul-climbing the moderate exit ramps when the leader slipped. The leader had just downclimbed to adjust his highest piece, and the extra slack added to the force of his fall. All three pieces he'd placed pulled out, and suddenly both men were tumbling toward the base of the cliff, more than 1,000 feet below. Yet something stopped them.

A Las Vegas Metropolitan Police SAR team responded via helicopter, flying with night vision equipment. Locating the climbers with a spotlight, they realized to their amazement that the climbers' rope had snagged on a tiny rock knob—this was all that was keeping them on the face. After picking up a bolt kit, rescuer Ben Williams and a police officer were flown to the slabby face and dropped off on a small ledge. Williams quickly drilled an anchor, lowered down, and very carefully clipped the stranded climbers' rope into the new anchor. After backing everything up, rescuers belayed and raised the two climbers to the anchor, from which they were flown to safety.

DATA TABLES

These tables include data from all accidents in the United States and Canada that are reported in this book, plus additional accidents for which data were available. Many climbing accidents each year are not reported. [*For 2021, fewer reports than usual were received from New York, Canada, and certain other areas.*] Therefore, these tables should not be viewed as precise counts of annual climbing accidents, and the data may not represent trends completely accurately. Readers likely will find the most value in the distribution and patterns of accident demographics and causes in Tables II and III.

TABLE I: REPORTED CLIMBING ACCIDENTS*

Year	Accidents Reported		Injured		Fatalities	
	US	CAN	US	CAN	US	CAN
1950s	33	n/a	26	n/a	10	n/a
1960s	66	8	52	7	21	3
1970s	114	18	97	10	34	8
1980s	191	29	124	26	33	8
1990	136	25	125	24	24	4
1991	169	20	147	11	18	6
1992	175	17	144	11	43	6
1993	132	27	121	17	21	1
1994	158	25	131	25	27	5
1995	168	24	134	18	37	7
1996	139	28	100	16	31	6
1997	158	35	148	24	31	13
1998	138	24	138	18	20	1
1999	123	29	91	20	17	10
2000	150	23	121	23	24	7
2001	150	22	138	14	16	2
2002	139	27	105	23	34	6
2003	118	29	105	22	18	6
2004	160	35	140	16	35	14
2005	111	19	85	14	34	7
2006	109	n/a	89	n/a	21	n/a
2007	113	n/a	95	n/a	15	n/a
2008	112	n/a	96	n/a	19	n/a
2009	126	n/a	112	n/a	23	n/a
2010	185	n/a	151	n/a	34	n/a
2011	157	n/a	109	n/a	29	n/a
2012	140	15	121	12	30	2
2013	143	11	100	5	21	4
2014	112	10	89	8	28	1

Year	Accidents Reported		Injured		Fatalities	
	US	CAN	US	CAN	US	CAN
2015	173	20	111	16	37	4
2016	175	23	134	17	32	6
2017	162	24	116	19	34	2
2018	187	17	198	12	17	5
2019	202	18	148	12	31	9
2020	157	19	118	13	28	5
2021	149	11	133	8	28	4
TOTAL	**8,513**	**1,126**	**7,078**	**837**	**1,800**	**334**

* Table I was revised in 2021. The figures presented for the 1950s, 1960s, 1970s, and 1980s are averages of the annual totals for each decade. The category "Total Persons Involved" has been eliminated. The "Total" figures are comprehensive totals from 1951 through 2021. The complete Table I from 1951 to 2019 is archived at publications.americanalpineclub.org.

TABLE II: REPORTED ACCIDENTS BY LOCATION*

Canada*	1959–2020		2021		
Geographic Districts	Accidents	Deaths	Accidents	Deaths	Injured
Alberta	613	163	8	4	6
British Columbia	365	136	3	0	2
Yukon & Northwest Territories	46	30	0	0	0
Ontario	43	9	0	0	0
Québec	34	10	0	0	0
Eastern Provinces & Territories	9	2	0	0	0

United States*	1951–2020		2021		
Geographic Districts	Accidents	Deaths	Accidents	Deaths	Injured
Alaska	669	229	21	5	21
Arizona, Nevada, Texas	148	27	6	1	5
Northeast	1303	171	7	1	6
Southeast	305	46	11	1	10
California	1700	354	23	2	25
Central	151	19	1	1	1
Colorado	1097	272	31	7	25
Montana, Idaho, South Dakota	121	46	4	0	4
Oregon	310	137	9	2	7
Utah, New Mex.	279	80	9	2	7
Washington	2096	359	11	2	9
Wyoming	687	168	16	4	13

* The Canada section of Table II was revised in 2021. Eastern Provinces and Territories includes Nunavut, Newfoundland, and the Maritimes. In the U.S., Northeast includes New England and the Mid-Atlantic states (southward to Maryland/Delaware), plus Ohio and Indiana. Southeast includes West Virginia, Virginia, Kentucky, and states farther south. Central incudes Michigan and the Upper Midwest (minus South Dakota), plus Missouri and Arkansas.

	1951–2020 USA	1959–2020 CAN*	2021 USA	2021 CAN
Terrain				
Rock	5885	633	107	9
Snow	2838	388	36	1
Ice	334	32	3	1
Water	26	3	0	0
Unknown	30	12	3	0
Ascent or Descent				
Ascent	4650	675	87	6
Descent	1649	426	34	4
Unknown	400	19	11	0
Other[1]	65	8	18	1
Climbing Style[†]				
Alpine/Mountaineering	108	13	47	5
Ice and mixed climbing	6	3	4	1
Traditional rock climbing	120	7	47	4
Sport climbing	56	5	27	1
Big-wall climbing	4	0	4	0
Bouldering	10	1	4	1
Top-rope	5	0	5	0
Free solo or DWS	9	2	2	0
Ski mountaineering	12	1	5	0
Other/Not Applicable/Unknown	26	1	6	0
Rope Position[†]				
Leading	106	10	41	3
Seconding	7	0	0	0
Top-roping	2	0	5	0
Roped but not belayed	6	0	2	2
Unroped	72	7	40	3
Rappelling	32	2	10	2
Lowering	15	0	6	0
Belaying	10	3	8	0
Other/Not Applicable/Unknown	84	13	37	2

[†]   "Climbing Style" and "Rope Position" categories were introduced in 2021. (The first two columns for each category include data from 2019 and 2020.) "Rope Position" tabulates the position or activity of the person(s) most directly affected by an accident (injured or killed, stranded, near miss, etc.), at the time the incident occurred. "Roped but not belayed" includes simul-climbing and glacier travel. "Unroped" includes bouldering.

	1951–2020 USA	1959–2020 CAN*	2021 USA	2021 CAN
Immediate Causes**				
Fall on rock	4440	343	62	5
Fall on ice (formerly snow or ice)	1257	228	1	0
Fall on snow	33	1	8	0
Falling rock, ice, object	747	157	16	1
Illness	475	28	7	0
Stranded / Lost	474	69	15	1
Avalanche	346	143	7	2
Rappel Failure/Error[3]	462	63	7	2
Lowering Error[6]	46	3	6	0
Fall from anchor	3	0	1	0
Anchor failure	11	1	2	0
Exposure	291	14	5	0
Glissade error	249	18	0	0
Protection pulled out	394	0	0	0
Failure to follow route	262	36	0	0
Fall into crevasse/moat	200	53	2	0
Faulty use of crampons	128	7	0	0
Ascending too fast	88	0	2	0
Skiing[4]	93	16	1	0
Lightning	69	7	0	0
Equipment failure	19	3	0	0
Other[5]	653	44	9	0
Unknown	120	15	1	0
Contributing Causes***				
Climbing unroped	1148	179	13	0
Inexperience	1128	211	11	0
Placed no/inadequate protection	966	115	0	1
Inadequate equipment/clothing	800	79	1	0
Weather	557	84	4	0
Climbing alone	486	75	0	0
No helmet	418	77	2	0
Inadequate belay	335	31	2	0
Protection pulled out (climber placed)	34	2	7	2
Protection pulled out (fixed)	4	0	0	0
Inadequate knot	6	0	0	0
Inadequate backup	16	0	1	0
Rope too short	3	0	1	1

	1951–2020 USA	1959–2020 CAN*	2021 USA	2021 CAN
Poor position	282	37	5	0
Darkness	195	23	2	1
Party separated	148	12	0	0
Loose rock/failure to test holds	165	57	15	1
Off-route	159	22	1	0
Failure to self-arrest	12	0	2	0
Exposure	70	16	4	0
Illness	49	10	10	0
Equipment failure	28	8	0	0
Other	365	106	23	4
Age of Individuals				
Under 15	1255	12	2	0
15-20	1381	206	3	0
21-25	1725	264	20	0
26-30	1644	223	16	5
31-35	2255	23	26	0
36-50	3652	152	22	0
Over 50	510	40	20	1
Unknown	2552	643	52	6
Sex[6]				
Male	787	89	107	6
Female	236	20	25	1
Not known	161	28	28	5
Experience Level				
Novice	2026	311	5	0
Intermediate	1919	367	47	4
Expert	2765	531	67	3
Unknown	3021	641	33	5
Month				
January	287	28	10	0
February	279	63	6	1
March	426	82	12	0
April	534	46	11	0
May	1122	75	24	2
June	1404	89	26	2
July	2213	284	14	1
August	1299	220	14	3
September	2137	87	10	1

	1951–2020 USA	1959–2020 CAN*	2021 USA	2021 CAN
October	589	44	7	1
November	290	25	8	0
December	150	29	5	0
Unknown	109	3	2	0

Type of Injury/Illness (Data since 1984. Fracture and internal injury breakouts introduced in 2020.)

	1951–2020 USA	1959–2020 CAN*	2021 USA	2021 CAN
Fracture: lower extremity	79	9	32	2
Fracture: upper extremity	16	4	4	0
Fracture: other	39	2	3	0
Spine injury/fracture	28	3	14	0
Total Fractures	1984	279	53	2
Laceration	932	91	5	1
Abrasion	485	80	6	0
Bruise	657	91	4	0
Sprain/Strain	519	38	14	0
Head Injury/TBI	461	41	10	3
Internal: chest	9	0	2	0
Internal: abdomen	2	0	2	0
Hypothermia	192	20	5	0
Frostbite	168	13	4	0
Dislocation	194	17	0	0
Puncture	70	14	1	0
Acute mountain sickness	57	0	0	0
HAPE	101	1	7	0
HACE	41	1	2	0
Other[7]	522	66	32	4
None	456	209	10	2

* No Canada data from 2006–2011; includes new data from 2012–2020

** "Fall on snow" and "anchor failure" were new in 2021 (past years combined falls on snow and ice). "Protection pulled out" combines two former categories; in this section, the protection pulling out must directly cause the fall.

*** Categories introduced in 2021 include "Protection pulled out (climber placed)" and "Protection pulled out (fixed)"; these replaced "Nut/cam pulled out" and "Piton/ice screw pulled out." Other new categories in 2021 were "Inadequate knot," "Inadequate backup," "Rope too short," and "Failure to self-arrest."

[1] Some reported accidents happen when climbers are at the top or bottom of a route, during an approach, or in camp. This category was created in 2001. The category "unknown" primarily reflects solo climbers.

[2] These are illnesses/injuries that led directly or indirectly to an accident or rescue, such as HAPE.

[3] Prior years included some lowering errors, anchor failures, and inadequate backups (now their own categories).

[4] This category covers ski mountaineering. Backcountry ski touring or snowshoeing incidents, including those involving avalanches, are not counted in these tables.

[5] These included belayer pulled into climbing wall, leg stuck in crack, ledge collapsed, and others.

[6] Categories introduced in 2016.

[7] These included crushing injuries, rope burns, and amputations. Note: Injuries are counted only once in each category for a given incident. For example, an accident that results in two broken ankles will be listed once under "Fracture: lower extremity."

CLIMBERS HELPING CLIMBERS SINCE 1959.

Alison Sheets.

MOUNTAIN RESCUE

MOUNTAIN
RESCUE
ASSOCIATION

We Never Charge for Rescue

Courage. Commitment. Compassion.

www.mra.org